The Little Book of
Country Baking

Classic Recipes for Cakes, Cookies, Breads, and Pies

Abigail R. Gehring

Skyhorse Publishing

Skyhorse Publishing books may be purchased in bulk at special discounts for sales promotion, corporate gifts, fund-raising, or educational purposes. Special editions can also be created to specifications. For details, contact the Special Sales Department, Skyhorse Publishing, 307 West 36th Street, 11th Floor, New York, NY 10018 or info@skyhorsepublishing.com.

Skyhorse® and Skyhorse Publishing® are registered trademarks of Skyhorse Publishing, Inc.®, a Delaware corporation.

Visit our website at www.skyhorsepublishing.com.

10 9 8 7 6 5 4 3 2 1

Library of Congress Cataloging-in-Publication Data is available on file.
ISBN: 978-1-61608-689-3

Printed in China

contents

INTRODUCTION

The irony of this cookbook is that when I bake, I cannot make myself stick to a recipe. Something in my independent nature resists following someone else's prescription for what I consider a very creative activity. I'll look to a recipe for inspiration, but I'll always add a little something to make it my own, or substitute an item or two out of necessity or pure curiosity. I encourage you to treat these recipes the same way: as guidelines for your own creative culinary ventures. If I don't specify what type of flour to use, all-purpose flour will yield the best results, but you can experiment with any of the myriad flours available at supermarkets and health food stores. Almost any fruit or nut in a recipe can be substituted with another fruit or nut, or omitted completely. Likewise, in most cases flavorings such as vanilla extract can be substituted with peppermint, orange, or any other flavoring you fancy. Here are just a few tips for happy experimentation.

Substituting Sweeteners: Sugar turns to a liquid as it bakes, helping cookies to spread and adding moisture to cakes and breads. Reducing the sugar in a recipe will change the texture of the end product, but this doesn't necessarily mean it will be bad—just different. If you want to use honey, agave, or maple syrup instead of white or brown sugar, use about ¾ cup to 1 cup sugar called for in the recipe, and reduce other liquids in the recipe by 2 to 3 tablespoons. And while we're on the subject, if a recipe calls for maple syrup, please only use the real deal!

Substituting Butter: Don't use margarine—it's not good for you and it won't yield good results. If you want to reduce the fat content of a cookie, cake, or bread recipe, you can experiment with substituting ¾ cup of canola oil per 1 cup of butter called for, or you can try using fruit purees (apple or prune), or a combination of the two.

Gluten-Free Baking: About two years ago I discovered, as more and more folks are, that my body doesn't like gluten. Fortunately, it's fairly easy to find gluten-free all-purpose flour mix now. But if you want to mix your own, I've included a recipe on the next page.

GLUTEN-FREE ALL-PURPOSE FLOUR MIX

1 cup sorghum flour

½ cup millet, almond, brown rice, quinoa, or buckwheat flour

1 cup tapioca, potato starch, or corn starch

1 teaspoon xanthan gum

Don't skip the xanthan gum—it's expensive and it sounds weird, but it will make a big difference in the texture of your baked good.

Note that some kinds of baking powder contain gluten, so read the labels. Also, adding a bit more butter or a bit of applesauce, pumpkin puree, prune paste, or yogurt to your recipes will help ensure the end product isn't too dry. Coconut flour is delicious, but add a little extra liquid when using it.

Happy baking!

Cookies and Bars

BROWN SUGAR COOKIES

Yields three to four dozen cookies

2 cups brown sugar	½ tsp salt
1 cup softened margarine	1 tsp baking soda
3 eggs	¼ cup milk
5 cups pastry flour	1 tsp vanilla extract

Preheat oven to 400° F.

Cream together the margarine and sugar. Beat the eggs well and add to the mixture. Add milk, vanilla, and half the flour sifted with the salt and soda. Add more flour, enough to make dough that may be rolled. Cut in any desired shapes and bake about 10 minutes.

Country Kitchen Tip

Many beloved old recipes have vague instructions for oven temperatures. Here's a handy guide:

Very moderate = 300°F to 350°F
Moderate/Medium = 350°F to 400°F
Hot/Quick/Fast = 400°F to 450°F
Very Hot/Very Quick = 450°F to 500°F

CHOCOLATE ALMOND COOKIES

Yields three dozen cookies

3 cups brown sugar

4 eggs

2 tsp cinnamon

½ tsp ground cloves

2 squares melted chocolate (16 oz)

½ lb chopped blanched almonds

2 cups chocolate chips

1 Tbs melted butter

2 tsp baking powder

1 cup whole wheat flour (plus extra
to stiffen dough)

Preheat oven to 400°F.

Beat eggs well, then add brown sugar and melted butter. Sift together one cup of whole wheat flour with cinnamon, cloves, and baking powder. Add to the mixture. Then add the melted chocolate, almonds, chocolate chips, and enough additional flour to make the dough stiff enough to shape in the hands. Roll in small balls. Place in greased pans not too close together. Bake about ten minutes.

Cookies and Bars

FRUIT AND NUT COOKIES

Yields four dozen cookies

1 ½ cups sugar
1 cup butter
3 eggs
1 Tbs cinnamon
½ tsp salt
3 cups flour

1 tsp baking soda, dissolved in 4 Tbs hot
    water
3 cups flour
1 cup raisins
1 cup currants
1 cup pistachios or almonds, broken up
1 tsp vanilla extract

Preheat oven to 300°F.

Cream together the butter, sugar, eggs, and vanilla. In a separate bowl, combine cinnamon, soda mixture, flour, fruits, and nuts. Add to butter mixture and mix thoroughly. Drop by spoonful onto greased pans. Bake for 23 to 25 minutes, or until slightly golden.

SOUR CREAM COOKIES

Yields three dozen cookies

1 cup sugar
½ cup butter
2 eggs
½ cup sour cream or sour milk

½ tsp baking soda
½ tsp salt
2 tsp grated nutmeg
2 cups flour, or as little as possible

Preheat oven to 350°F.

Cream the butter, then add the sugar and cream again. Sift together one cup flour, baking soda, salt, and nutmeg. To the creamed mixture, add the eggs well beaten, sour cream, and the sifted mixture. Add the rest of the flour. Roll out to one-third of an inch thickness, cut any desired shape, and place on baking sheets. Bake for 10 to 15 minutes or until set. Sugar mixed with a little flour may be sifted over the dough before cutting. Raisins may also be pressed into the top of each cookie.

Country Kitchen Tip

Always break eggs into a separate cup or bowl before adding them to your dough or batter.

DROP COOKIES

Yields 2 dozen cookies

⅓ cups butter

1 cup sugar

1 egg

½ cup sour milk

½ tsp baking soda

¼ tsp salt

1 tsp vanilla extract

¼ cup chopped raisins

2 ½ cups flour

½ tsp baking powder

Preheat oven to 350°F.

Cream the butter, add the sugar, and then add the whole egg. Mix well. Add the sour milk and the vanilla. In a separate bowl, mix the baking powder, soda, salt, and flour well, add the raisins, and then add to the first mixture. Beat well. Drop from a spoon onto a buttered and floured pan, leaving three inches between the cookies. Bake approximately 10 to 15 minutes.

CHOCOLATE COOKIES

Yields three dozen cookies

1 cup sugar

⅓ cup butter

1 egg

¼ cup milk

2 cups flour

½ tsp cinnamon

½ tsp salt

3 tsp baking powder

1 square chocolate (8 oz), melted

1 tsp vanilla

Preheat oven to 325°F.

Cream the butter, then add the sugar and cream well. Add alternately egg beaten in milk and sifted flour, cinnamon, salt, and baking powder. Add the chocolate and vanilla. Turn out on a floured board and roll a small portion at a time to one-fourth of an inch in thickness. Cut with a floured cookie cutter. Place on a buttered, floured pan and bake about 10 minutes or until slightly brown.

WALNUT COOKIES

Yields 3 dozen cookies

⅓ cup butter
⅔ cup sugar
1 egg
4 Tbs milk
2 cups flour
2 tsp baking powder

⅓ cups chopped walnuts (other nuts can
be used as substitute)
1 tsp cinnamon
¼ tsp cloves
¼ tsp mace
¼ tsp nutmeg

Preheat oven to 350°F.

Cream the butter, then add the sugar and mix well. Add the egg and milk, and then the flour, nuts, cinnamon, cloves, mace, nutmeg, and baking powder. Place the dough on a floured board. Roll it out one-fourth of an inch thick and cut with a cookie cutter. Place on a well-buttered and floured baking sheet. Bake approximately twelve minutes. Frost with Confectioner's Sugar Icing if desired (page 180).

SUGAR COOKIES

Yields 4 dozen cookies

2 cups sugar
1 cup butter
2 eggs, whites and yolks beaten sepa-
    rately
1 tsp baking powder

4 cups flour (approximately—add as
    needed to stiffen dough)
1 tsp salt
1 tsp vanilla extract

Preheat oven to 350°F.

Cream butter, sugar, and vanilla together. Add well-beaten yolks of the eggs, then the whites, then sift in baking powder, flour, and salt mixture. Roll out flat, cut out with cookie cutters, and bake on greased cookie sheet for 6-8 minutes. Sprinkle with coarse sugar or, when cool, frost with Confectioner's Sugar Icing (page 180).

PEANUT COOKIES

Yields 1 to 2 dozen cookies

2 Tbs butter   ¼ tsp salt
2 Tbs milk   ½ cup flour
1 tsp baking powder   ½ cup chopped peanuts
¼ cup sugar   ½ tsp vanilla extract
1 egg

Preheat oven to 350°F.

Cream together the butter, sugar, and egg. Add the milk and vanilla continue to beat. In a separate bowl, combine the dry ingredients and then add to the butter mixture, mixing thoroughly. Add peanuts. Drop from a teaspoon on unbuttered sheets one inch apart. Bake for approximately 10 minutes.

BUTTERSCOTCH COOKIES

Yields 4 dozen cookies

2 cups medium brown sugar
1 cup butter, softened
1 Tbs vinegar
2 eggs

1 tsp vanilla extract
2 ½ cups flour
1 Tbs baking soda
1 Tbs cream of tartar

Preheat oven to 375°F.

Cream together the butter and brown sugar. In a separate bowl, mix together flour, baking soda, and cream of tartar. Mix together eggs, vanilla, and vinegar. And add to the butter mixture alternately with the flour mixture. Form dough into a long roll and wrap tightly in plastic wrap. Refrigerate overnight. In the morning, slice the roll into ½-inch slices and place on greased cookie sheet. Bake for 10 to 12 minutes or until the edges are slightly browned.

Country Kitchen Tip

Don't have brown sugar on hand? Combine 1 cup granulated sugar and 2 tablespoons molasses per 1 cup of brown sugar called for in the recipe.

OATMEAL COOKIES

Yields 3 dozen cookies

2 Tbs butter   2 cups oats
1 cup sugar   1 tsp vanilla
2 eggs   2 tsp baking powder

Preheat oven to 375°F.

Cream together the butter and sugar until light and fluffy. Add eggs and vanilla and beat. Add oats and baking powder and mix thoroughly. Drop by teaspoonfuls on well-greased cookie sheets. Bake for 8 to 10 minutes, or until slightly golden. Allow them to stand several minutes before removing from the pans.

DATE BARS

Yields 1 dozen bars

1 cup nuts	1 tsp baking powder
1 cup dates	1 tsp vanilla
2 eggs	¾ cup powdered sugar
3 Tbs flour	2 Tbs heavy cream

Preheat oven to 350°F.

Combine nuts, dates, flour, baking powder, and vanilla. Beat eggs separately and add. Add powdered sugar and heavy cream. Turn dough into a greased 8 x 10 baking pan and bake for approximately 20 minutes or until edges are golden brown.

CHOCOLATE JUMBLES

Yields 3 to 4 dozen cookies

2 cups sugar
3 eggs
1 cup butter, softened
2 squares melted chocolate (16 oz)

1 tsp baking soda dissolved in
   2 Tbs warm water
4 cups flour

Preheat oven to 350°F.

Cream together the butter and sugar. Add the eggs and melted chocolate and continue to beat. Combine dry ingredients separately and add to the butter mixture along with the baking soda and water. Roll into balls and place on lightly greased cookie sheet, flattening them slightly. Bake for 10 to 12 minutes.

MOLASSES COOKIES

Yields 2 to 3 dozen cookies

1 cup brown sugar
⅔ cup molasses
½ cup butter
½ cup hot water
1 egg

1 tsp ginger
2 tsp baking soda
1/8 tsp salt
2 cups flour (approximately—add as
    needed to stiffen dough)

Preheat oven to 375°F.

Cream together the butter, brown sugar, and molasses. Add egg and continue to beat. In a separate bowl, combine dry ingredients. Add to the butter mixture along with the water. Roll dough into walnut sized balls and place onto well-greased baking sheets. Bake for 8 to 10 minutes, or until tops of cookies are cracked.

WALNUT MACAROONS

Yields 1 to 2 dozen macaroons

¼ lb walnuts   2 egg whites
¼ lb sugar

Preheat oven to 375°F.

In a food processor fitted with a steel blade, grind the walnuts with the sugar until the mixture resembles coarse crumbs. Beat egg whites until stiff and fold in dry mixture. Shape with a spoon and bake on unbuttered parchment paper for 12 to 15 minutes or until the tops are golden and slightly cracked.

OATMEAL CHOCOLATE CHIP COOKIES

Yields about 3 dozen cookies

1 ½ cups old-fashioned rolled oats
½ cup unsalted butter, softened
½ cup granulated sugar
½ cup light brown sugar, firmly packed
1 egg
1 tsp vanilla extract

1 cup flour
½ tsp baking powder
½ tsp baking soda
¼ tsp salt
12 oz semisweet chocolate chips

Preheat oven to 375°F.

Place the oats in a food processor and process until fine. Combine ground oats with the flour, baking powder, baking soda, and salt. In a separate bowl, cream together the butter and sugar until light and fluffy. Add egg and vanilla and continue to beat. Add the oat mixture to the butter mixture and mix thoroughly. Finally, add the chocolate chips. Drop the dough by spoonfuls onto the ungreased baking sheets and bake until golden brown, about 10 minutes. Cool slightly on the sheets before removing.

BROWNIES

Yields about 16 brownies

½ cup butter
2 squares unsweetened baking chocolate
(16 oz)
1 cup sugar

2 eggs
1 tsp vanilla extract
1 tsp baking powder
½ cup flour

Preheat oven to 350°F.

In a saucepan over low heat, melt the butter and chocolate, stirring constantly. Remove from heat, and allow to cool slightly. Add the eggs, slightly beaten, and the vanilla. Combine the dry ingredients separately and then add to the chocolate mixture. Pour batter into a greased 8-inch square baking pan and bake for about 20 minutes or until a toothpick inserted into the center comes out mostly clean. Bake a shorter time for gooey brownies, longer for cake-like brownies.

CHOCOLATE ALMOND BISCOTTI

Yields about 2 dozen biscotti

2 cups flour
½ cup almonds
1 cup sugar
¼ cup cocoa powder
1 tsp baking soda
½ tsp salt

¼ cup chocolate chips
2 eggs
2 egg whites
1 egg white mixed with 1 tsp water
2 tsp orange zest
1 tsp vanilla

Preheat oven to 350°F.

In a large mixing bowl, combine all dry ingredients. In a separate bowl, whisk together the eggs, egg whites, vanilla, and orange zest. Add wet ingredients to dry ingredients and mix thoroughly. Add almonds and chocolate chips.

Divide dough in half and roll into two 14-inch logs. Place far apart on a greased cookie sheet. Brush the logs with egg white and water mixture. Bake for 25 minutes, allow to cool, and then slice the biscotti at a 45-degree angle. Bake for another 7 minutes, cut sides down. Turn all biscotti over, and bake another 7 minutes. Store in an airtight container.

CINNAMON TWISTS

Yields about 4 dozen twists

3 cups flour
2 tsp baking powder
1 cup sugar

¾ cup oil
3 eggs
½ cup cinnamon-sugar

Preheat oven to 350°F.

Mix together the flour and baking powder. Combine eggs, sugar, and oil, and add to dry ingredients. Use your hands, dipped in flour, to roll pieces of dough into long rolls about the thickness of pencils. Twist into figure eights, dip in cinnamon-sugar, and place on a lightly greased cookie sheet. Bake for 10 to 12 minutes.

GINGER CREAMS

Yields 6 dozen cookies

4 ¼ cups flour
2 tsp baking soda
2 tsp ginger
1 tsp nutmeg
1 tsp cloves
1 tsp cinnamon
½ tsp salt

½ cup butter, softened
1 cup sugar
1 egg
1 cup molasses
⅔ cup hot water
Brown Sugar Icing (see page 179)

Preheat oven to 350°F.

Mix together flour, baking soda, spices, and salt. In a separate bowl, cream together butter and sugar. Add egg and beat. Add dry ingredients alternately with molasses and hot water, beating after each addition. Chill dough for about an hour. Drop by teaspoonfuls onto greased baking sheets and bake for 9 to 12 minutes. Cool cookies on baking racks. Frost with Brown Sugar Icing.

HALVAH SHORTBREAD

Yields about 16 cookies

¾ cup butter
½ cup tahini
⅛ tsp salt

1 ¼ cup brown sugar
2 cups pastry flour
½ cup toasted pecans, ground

Preheat oven to 375°F.

Cream together the butter, tahini, salt, and brown sugar. Add flour and mix thoroughly. Add nuts. Turn stiff batter into two well-greased 7-inch pie plates. Press the dough down to cover the bottoms of the pans evenly. Bake for 15 minutes or until edges become golden brown. Cut into wedges while still warm.

EASY CARAMEL ROLLS

Yields approximately 9 rolls

2 cups flour
4 tsp baking powder
1 tsp salt
½ cup butter
⅓ cup milk

⅓ cup water
1 cup light brown sugar
2 Tbs butter
Nutmeg

Preheat oven to 375°F.

Mix together the flour, baking powder, and salt. Work in 1/2 cup butter with the tips of the fingers until it is thoroughly blended. Add the milk and water, and mix to a soft dough. Dust a large cutting board with flour and roll out the dough to one-fourth inch thickness.

Cream the brown sugar and 2 Tbs butter together until smooth, then spread lightly over the dough. Roll up the dough like a jelly roll, fasten end by moistening with milk or water, and cut in pieces three-fourths inch thick. Sprinkle just a little nutmeg over each slice and bake on a greased cookie sheet for 15 minutes. Serve hot.

Breads, Muffins, and Scones

DATE-ORANGE BREAD

Yields 1 tea loaf

2 Tbs butter, melted
¾ cup orange juice
2 Tbs grated orange rind
½ cup finely cut dates
1 cup sugar
1 egg, slightly beaten

½ cup coarsely chopped pecans
2 cups sifted all-purpose flour
½ tsp baking soda
1 tsp baking powder
½ tsp salt

Preheat oven to 350°F.

Combine first seven ingredients. Mix and sift remaining ingredients; stir in. Mix well, but quickly, being careful not to overbeat.

Turn into greased loaf pan. Bake for 50 minutes or until a toothpick inserted into the center comes out clean. Remove from pan and let cool right side up on a wire rack.

CRANBERRY COFFEE CAKE

Yields about 6 servings

2 Tbs butter

¼ cup firmly packed brown sugar

1 cup cooked or canned cranberry sauce

¼ cup pecans, chopped

1 Tbs grated orange rind

1 ½ cups sifted flour

2 tsp double acting baking powder

¼ cup sugar

⅓ cup butter

1 beaten egg

½ cup milk

Preheat oven to 400°F.

Melt butter in 9-inch ring mold. Spread brown sugar over bottom of pan. Combine cranberry sauce, pecans, and orange rind. Spread over brown sugar in bottom of pan.

Sift together flour, baking powder, and sugar. Cut in butter until dough resembles coarse meal. Combine egg with milk. Add all at once, mixing only to dampen flour. Turn into pan.

Bake for 25 to 30 minutes. Cool 5 minutes and invert onto plate. Serve warm.

PINEAPPLE NUT BREAD

Yields 1 tea loaf

2 ¼ cups sifted flour
¾ cup sugar
1 ½ tsp salt
3 tsp baking powder
½ tsp baking soda

1 cup prepared bran cereal
¾ cup chopped walnuts
1 ½ cups crushed pineapple, undrained
1 egg beaten
3 Tbs butter, melted

Preheat oven to 350°F.

Sift flour, sugar, salt, baking powder, and soda together. Mix together remaining ingredients and combine with dry mixture. Bake in greased loaf pan for 1 ¼ hrs. This bread keeps moist for seven to ten days, and slices best when a day or more old.

BERRY LOAF

Yields 1 tea loaf

⅓ cup butter
⅔ cup brown sugar
⅓ cup buttermilk
1 egg
1 ½ cups all-purpose flour
1 tsp baking powder

½ tsp baking soda
½ tsp cinnamon
½ tsp salt
½ tsp nutmeg
1 cup berries, rinsed and drained

Preheat oven to 350°F.

Grease and lightly flour a bread pan.

Cream together the butter and brown sugar. In a separate bowl, combine all the dry ingredients thoroughly. Whisk together the buttermilk and egg and add to the brown sugar and butter mixture a little at a time, alternating with the dry ingredients. Do not over mix. Add the berries, mix lightly, and pour into the greased bread pan.

Bake for 50 to 60 minutes, or until a toothpick inserted into the loaf comes out clean.

Breads, Muffins, and Scones

COCOA MUFFINS

Yields 12 muffins

2 Tbs butter   ¼ tsp salt
1 cup sugar   ½ cup milk
2 Tbs cocoa powder   1 ½ cup all-purpose flour
½ teaspoon cinnamon   2 eggs, separated
3 tsp baking powder   ½ tsp vanilla

Preheat oven to 400°F.

Grease a 12-cup muffin tin, or line with paper cupcake liners.

Cream together the butter and sugar. Add egg yolks and beat until light and fluffy. In a separate bowl, combine flour, cocoa, salt, cinnamon, and baking powder; add alternately with the milk to the butter, sugar, and egg mixture. Add vanilla.

Beat egg whites with the salt until they form stiff peaks. Fold into batter.

Fill muffin cups two-thirds full and bake for about 17 to 23 minutes or until a toothpick inserted into the center comes out clean.

MAPLE ROLLS

Yields approximately 9 rolls

2 cups flour
4 tsp baking powder
1 tsp salt
¾ cup milk
2 Tbs butter

½ cup granulated maple sugar (or ⅓ cup
     light brown sugar and ¼ cup real
     maple syrup)
2 Tbs melted butter

Preheat oven to 350°F.

Combine the flour, baking powder, and salt. Use a fork to mix in the butter. Add the milk and combine. Dust a flat surface with flour and roll the dough into a rectangle shape one-half inch thick. Brush the dough with the melted butter and spread with the maple sugar. Dampen the outer edges with a little cold water and roll up firmly. Cut in crosswise slices about one-half inch thick, place in a well-greased baking pan, cut side down, and bake for 20 to 25 minutes.

APPLE CORN BREAD

Yields 9 servings

1 cup cornmeal
½ cup bread flour
1 tsp salt
1 Tbs molasses
¾ cup buttermilk

½ tsp baking powder
1 Tbs butter, softened
3 medium-sized apples
½ tsp baking soda

Preheat oven to 350°F.

Mix all the dry ingredients thoroughly together; add the buttermilk, molasses, and butter, and mix well. Pour into a shallow 8 x 8 greased baking pan, and place the apples, peeled and thinly sliced, over the top. Bake for 45 minutes or until a toothpick inserted into the center comes out clean. Remove from oven, cool, and dust with powdered sugar.

PEANUT BUTTER BREAD

Yields 1 tea loaf

½ cup peanut butter
½ cup sugar
1 egg, beaten
3 ½ cups bread flour

3 tsp baking powder
1 cup milk
½ tsp salt

Preheat oven to 350°F.

Cream together the peanut butter and sugar. Add the egg and beat until combined. Mix and sift the dry ingredients and add alternately with the milk. Beat the entire mixture well and pour into a well-greased loaf pan. Bake for 50 minutes or until a toothpick inserted into the center comes out clean.

RICE SPOON BREAD

Yields 1 tea loaf

2 cups cooked rice
3 eggs
1 cup cornmeal
4 cups milk

1 Tbs melted butter
4 tsp baking powder
3 tsp salt

Preheat oven to 350°F.

Beat the eggs lightly, and add the rice, milk, and butter. Sift the dry ingredients together, and add to the first mixture. Pour into a greased loaf pan and bake for 45 minutes.

SPOON BREAD

Yields 4 to 6 servings

2 cups milk

½ cup cornmeal

½ tsp baking powder

1 tsp salt

3 eggs, separated

Preheat oven to 350°F.

Heat the milk nearly to boiling. Stir in cornmeal gradually and cook until the consistency of mush. Add the baking powder, salt, and egg yolks, beaten until light. Beat the egg whites until stiff and fold into the batter. Pour into a greased 8-inch round baking dish and bake for 30 minutes or until a toothpick inserted into the center comes out clean. Serve while hot with plenty of butter.

PEANUT BREAD

Yields 1 tea loaf

2 cups flour
4 tsp baking powder
½ tsp salt
4 Tbs sugar

1 egg
½ cup chopped peanuts
¾ cup milk

Preheat oven to 375°F.

Combine the flour, baking powder, salt, sugar, and peanuts. Add the egg and milk. Stir vigorously for two minutes. Place in a well-buttered bread pan, and bake 35 minutes or until a toothpick inserted into the center comes out clean.

OLIVE BREAD

Yields 1 medium-sized loaf

1 ½ cups bread flour
1 ½ cups Graham flour
2 tsp baking powder
½ cup molasses

½ tsp baking soda
1 cup ripe olives
1 ¾ cups milk
1 ½ tsp salt

Preheat oven to 350°F.

Sift together flour, salt, and baking powder. Mix thoroughly. Add baking soda to the molasses, and combine with milk. Mix all together and beat well. Lastly, add the ripe olives, stoned and coarsely chopped, turn into a well-greased loaf-pan, and bake for 45 to 60 minutes, or until a toothpick inserted into the center comes out clean.

DATE MUFFINS

Yields 12 muffins

¼ cup sugar
¼ cup dates finely chopped
1 egg
¼ tsp salt

¾ cup milk
1 ¾ cups flour
4 tsp baking powder
2 Tbs butter, melted

Preheat oven to 375°F.

Mix together the sugar, dates, baking powder, flour, and salt. Whisk together milk and egg, and add to dry ingredients. Beat for two minutes. Add butter, melted. Fill well-greased muffin pans half full of the mixture and place in the oven. Bake for 20 to 25 minutes.

NUT BREAD

Yields 2 tea loaves

1 ½ cups Graham flour
2 cups white flour
4 tsp baking powder
1 cup light brown sugar

2 tsp salt
1 ½ cups milk
⅔ cup chopped nuts, dates, and/or raisins

Preheat oven to 375°F.

Sift together all the dry ingredients, and add the nuts and fruit. Add the milk. Stir well, and pour into two greased loaf pans. Allow to stand and rise for twenty minutes. Bake for 45 minutes, or until a toothpick inserted into the center comes out clean.

OLD-FASHIONED RUSK

Yields 1 tea loaf

1 cup sugar
1 egg
1 Tbs butter
2 ½ cups flour
1 tsp cinnamon
½ tsp cloves

½ tsp nutmeg
½ tsp salt
1 cup raisins
1 cup buttermilk
1 tsp baking soda

Preheat oven to 350°F.

Combine all ingredients except buttermilk. Add buttermilk, mix, and pour into greased loaf pan. Bake for 50 to 60 minutes, or until lightly golden.

Country Kitchen Tip

You can grind grains into flour at home using a mortar and pestle, a coffee or spice mill, manual or electric food grinders, a blender, or a food processor. Grains with a shell (quinoa, wheat berries, etc.) should be rinsed and dried before milling to remove the layer of resin from the outer shell that can impart a bitter taste to your flour. Rinse the grains thoroughly in a colander or mesh strainer, then spread them on a paper or cloth towel to absorb the extra moisture. Transfer to a baking sheet and allow to air dry completely (to speed this process you can put them in a very low oven for a few minutes). When the grains are dry, they're ready to be ground.

SQUASH MUFFINS

Yields 12 muffins

1 cup cooked and pureed squash
2 eggs
1 cup brown sugar
1 cup milk
¼ teaspoon salt

1 ½ cups all-purpose flour
1 tsp baking soda
1 tsp baking powder
1 teaspoon cinnamon
¼ cup vegetable oil

Preheat oven to 375°F.

Sift together all dry ingredients except sugar. Add the squash, eggs, sugar, milk, and oil and mix well. Fill well-greased or paper-lined muffin tins two-thirds full. Bake for 20 to 25 minutes.

MULTIGRAIN BREAD

Yields 1 loaf

¼ cup yellow cornmeal
¼ cup packed brown sugar
1 tsp salt
2 Tbs vegetable oil
1 cup boiling water

1 package active dry yeast
¼ cup warm (105 to 115°F) water
⅓ cup whole wheat flour
¼ cup rye flour
2 ¼–2 ¾ cups all-purpose flour

Mix cornmeal, brown sugar, salt, and oil with boiling water; cool to lukewarm (105 to 115°F). Dissolve yeast in ¼ cup warm water; stir into cornmeal mixture. Add whole wheat and rye flours and mix well. Stir in enough all-purpose flour to make dough stiff enough to knead.

Turn dough onto lightly floured surface. Knead until smooth and elastic, about 5 to 10 minutes. Place dough in lightly oiled bowl, turning to oil top. Cover with clean towel; let rise in warm place until double, about 1 hour.

Punch dough down; turn onto clean surface. Cover with clean towel; let rest 10 minutes. Shape dough and place in greased 9 x 5 pan. Cover with clean towel; let rise until almost double, about 1 hour.

Preheat oven to 375°F. Bake 35 to 45 minutes or until bread sounds hollow when tapped. Cover with aluminum foil during baking if bread is browning too quickly. Remove bread from pan and cool on wire rack.

SOUR CREAM BISCUITS

Yields about 10 biscuits

1 cup all-purpose flour
½ cup sour cream
¼ cup milk

1 tsp baking powder
½ tsp baking soda
⅓ tsp salt

Preheat oven to 450°F.

Sift the flour, baking powder, baking soda, and salt together in a mixing bowl. Add the sour cream and, when well mixed, the milk. Mix until smooth and roll out to about 1 inch thick, using as little flour on the board as possible. Use a round cookie cutter or an upside down glass to cut into circles, and place on an ungreased baking sheet. Bake for 12 minutes.

Country Kitchen Tip

Making good gluten-free bread. There are several things you can do to improve your chances of successful gluten-free bread baking:

• Choose flours that are high in protein, such as sorghum, amaranth, millet, teff, oatmeal, and buckwheat
• Use all room temperature ingredients. Yeast thrives in warm environments.
• Add a couple teaspoons of xantham gum to your dry ingredients.
• Add eggs and dry milk powder to your bread. These will add texture and help the bread to rise.
• Substitiute carbonated water or gluten-free beer for other liquids in the recipe.
• Add extra liquid (water, carbonated water, milk, fruit juice, or olive oil) to get a soft and sticky consistency. The batter should be a little too sticky to knead. For this reason, bread machines are great for making gluten-free bread.

OATMEAL BREAD

Yields 1 loaf

1 cup rolled oats
1 tsp salt
1 ½ cups boiling water
1 package active dry yeast
¼ cup warm water (105 to 115°F)

¼ cup light molasses
1 ½ Tbs vegetable oil
2 cups whole wheat flour
2–2 ½ cups all-purpose flour

Combine rolled oats and salt in a large mixing bowl. Stir in boiling water; cool to lukewarm (105 to 115°F).

Dissolve yeast in ¼ cup warm water in small bowl. Add yeast, water, molasses, and oil to cooled oatmeal mixture. Stir in whole wheat flour and 1 cup all-purpose flour. Add additional all-purpose flour to make the dough stiff enough to knead.

Knead dough on lightly floured surface until smooth and elastic, about 5 minutes. Place dough in lightly oiled bowl, turning to oil top. Cover with clean towel; let rise in warm place until double, about 1 hour.

Punch dough down; turn onto clean surface. Shape dough and place in greased 9 x 5 pan. Cover with clean towel; let rise in a warm place until almost double, about 1 hour.

Preheat oven to 375°F. Bake 50 minutes or until bread sounds hollow when tapped. Cover with aluminum foil during baking if bread is browning too quickly. Remove bread from pan and cool on wire rack.

RAISED BUNS (BRIOCHE)

Yields 12 to 18 buns

½ cup milk
⅓ cup butter
¼ cup sugar
¾ tsp salt
1 package yeast (active, dry, or
    compressed)

¼ cup lukewarm water
3 eggs, well beaten
2 ½ cups enriched flour
¼ tsp lemon rind, or ⅛ tsp crushed
    cardamom seeds

Save 2 tablespoons egg to brush brioches before baking. Scald milk; stir in butter, sugar, and salt, and cool to lukewarm. Sprinkle or crumble yeast into water in large bowl and stir to dissolve. Add lukewarm milk mixture and beaten eggs; mix well.

Sift flour; add 1 ½ cups of it to mixture and beat by hand 8 minutes or with electric mixer at medium speed 3 minutes. Add remaining sifted flour and lemon rind; beat to smooth, heavy batter. Cover with towel; let rise in warm place 2 hours or until doubled. Stir down, cover tightly, and chill at least 5 hours or overnight.

Stir down again. Mixture is soft now. Grease hands slightly, place dough on lightly floured board, and knead a few times. With sharp knife, cut off small pieces of dough. Roll with hands to about one-half inch in diameter, and about 10 inches long. Coil loosely in circle, winding around toward center. Top with small ball of dough.

Preheat oven to 400°F. Cover with a towel and let rise 30 minutes, or until doubled. Brush with egg yolk beaten with 1 teaspoon water. If desired, sprinkle with coarse sugar. Bake for 12 to 15 minutes. For an extra touch, top with thin frosting while still warm. Yields 12 to 18 buns.

LEMON GINGER SCONES

4 cups flour
1 cup sugar
2 teaspoons baking powder
¼ teaspoon cream of tartar
1 teaspoon salt
1 cup butter
1 egg

1 cup sour cream
1 teaspoon baking soda
1 tsp lemon juice
1 tsp lemon zest, grated
½ cup candied ginger, cut into small
    pieces

Preheat oven to 350°F.

In a large mixing bowl, combine the flour, sugar, baking powder, cream of tartar, and salt. Add the butter in small pieces and use fingers to mix until flour resembles small crumbs. In a separate small bowl, mix together the sour cream, baking soda, lemon juice, and lemon zest. Add to the flour mixture along with the egg (beaten slightly) and candied ginger and mix just until moistened.

On a lightly floured surface, knead the dough briefly. Form into a disk that's about three-quarters of an inch and use a glass dipped in flour or a round cookie cutter to cut into small disks. Bake on a greased cookie sheet for 12 to 15 minutes or until tops are golden.

Pies, Crumbles, and Crisps

BUTTER PECAN PIE

3 egg whites, beaten stiff
1 tsp baking powder
1 cup sugar
1 tsp vanilla

20 saltine crackers, coarsely broken
½ cup pecans, chopped
Whipped cream (for topping)

Preheat oven to 300°F.

Beat egg whites until stiff; add baking powder and beat another ten seconds or so. Add sugar and vanilla and beat until combined. Fold in crackers and pecans. Pour into buttered pie plate and bake for 30 minutes. Let cool, then top with whipped cream and chopped pecans.

CHOCOLATE-PECAN FUDGE PIE

1 ¼ cup chocolate wafer crumbs
⅓ cup butter, melted
½ cup butter, softened
¾ cup brown sugar
3 eggs
12 oz semisweet chocolate morsels
2 tsp instant coffee

1 tsp vanilla extract
½ cup flour
1 cup pecans, coarsely chopped
Whipped cream
Chocolate syrup
Maraschino cherries with stems
Mint sprigs

Combine chocolate wafer crumbs and ⅓ cup melted butter. Firmly press on bottom and sides of a 9-inch tart pan or pie plate. Bake at 350°F for 6 to 8 minutes.

Cream ½ cup softened butter. Gradually add brown sugar and continue to beat at medium speed until blended. Add the eggs, one at a time, beating after each addition. Melt the chocolate in a double boiler and stir into the butter-sugar mixture, along with the instant coffee granules, vanilla extract, flour, and chopped pecans. Pour into the prepared crust. Bake at 375°F for 25 minutes. Remove from oven and cool completely on a rack.

Just before serving, spread whipped cream over cooled pie and drizzle with chocolate syrup. Garnish with cherries and/or mint if desired.

DIVINE TRIPLE CHOCOLATE PIE

CHOCOLATE PIE CRUST

1 cup unbleached flour, sifted
¼ tsp salt
⅓ cup butter

½ oz semi-sweet chocolate, grated
2 Tbs cold water

FILLING

¼ cup sugar
1 envelope unflavored gelatin
¼ tsp salt
1 cup milk
3 large eggs, separated

3 oz baking chocolate, cut up
½ tsp vanilla
¼ tsp cream of tartar
¼ cup sugar
1 cup heavy cream, whipped

GARNISH

Sweetened whipped cream

½ oz semi-sweet chocolate

CHOCOLATE PIE CRUST

Sift the salt and flour into a bowl and cut in the butter, using a pastry blender, until coarse crumbs form. Add the chocolate and water, tossing with a fork, until the dough forms. Press the dough firmly into a ball and then roll out on a lightly floured surface into a 13-inch circle. Loosely fit the dough into a 9-inch pie plate and trim the edge so that it reaches 1 inch beyond the rim of the pie plate. Fold the extra under the edge of the crust to from a ridge. Flute the edge and prick the entire surface of the pie shell with a fork. Bake at 400°F for 12 minutes or until golden brown. Cool on a rack.

FILLING

Stir ¼ cup of sugar, gelatin, and salt together in a 2-quart saucepan. Stir in milk and slightly beaten egg yolks. Add baking chocolate and cook over low heat, stirring constantly, until the chocolate melts and the gelatin dissolves. Remove from the heat and stir in vanilla. Chill in the refrigerator, stirring occasionally, until the mixture is the consistency of unbeaten egg whites. Then remove the chocolate mixture from the refrigerator and set aside.

Beat egg whites and cream of tartar in another bowl, until foamy, using an electric mixer set on high speed. Gradually add ¼ cup of sugar, 1 Tbs at a time, beating well after each addition. Continue beating until stiff, glossy peaks form when the beaters are slowly lifted. When the chocolate mixture mounds slightly when dropped from a spoon, beat until smooth, using an electric mixer at medium speed. Fold the egg white mixture into the chocolate mixture; then fold in the whipped cream. Chill in the refrigerator until the mixture mounds well when spooned. Turn into the chocolate pie shell. Chill in the refrigerator for 2 hours or until set.

To serve, decorate with puffs of sweetened whipped cream. Grate and sprinkle the chocolate over the whipped cream.

MOCHA VELVET PIE

1 9-inch pie shell, pre-baked
½ cup butter
¾ cup sugar
1 square unsweetened baking chocolate
    (8 oz)

1 tsp vanilla
1 ½ Tbs instant coffee
2 eggs
½ cup whipping cream

Cream butter in medium-size bowl and gradually add sugar, creaming well after each addition. Melt chocolate in a double boiler and add to butter-sugar mixture, along with instant coffee and vanilla, continuing to beat. Add eggs, one at a time, beating for five minutes after each egg to make batter creamy, thick, and fluffy. Turn into baked pastry shell. Chill 1 to 2 hours. Whip the cream and top the cake with it just before serving.

NOTE: Consuming raw eggs may increase your risk of foodborne illness. Populations at particular risk include pregnant women, elderly, very young children, and individuals with compromised immune systems.

CHOCOLATE CARAMEL HAZELNUT PIE

1 9-inch pie shell, pre-baked

FILLING

1 ½ cups sugar

½ cup water

½ cup unsalted butter, cut into pieces

1 5-oz can evaporated milk

2 oz unsweetened chocolate, chopped

2 cups hazelnuts or filberts, skinned and
    coarsely chopped

OPTIONAL DECORATION

8 whole hazelnuts, skinned

24 sliced almonds

In a large, heavy-bottomed saucepan, stir together the sugar and water. Set the saucepan over medium-high heat. Let the sugar mixture come to a boil and continue to cook until it caramelizes. Do not stir the sugar as it cooks. If it caramelizes unevenly, you can move it around by swirling it in the pan. When the sugar is a rich golden brown, remove it from heat and stir in the butter and evaporated milk gradually, mixing well with a wooden spoon until smooth. Let cool for 5 minutes and stir in the chocolate. Beat with a whisk until very smooth. Set the filling aside to cool for 10 to 15 minutes and then stir in the nuts. Meanwhile, preheat the oven to 475°F.

Pour the filling into the pie shell and bake for 10 minutes, until the edge is very brown and the center is bubbling. Once the pie has cooled to room temperature, about 1 hour, decorate it, if desired, by making small flowers with the whole hazelnuts and sliced almonds.

MEXICAN MOCHA PIE

1 9-inch pie shell, pre-baked

1 envelope unflavored gelatin

⅓ cup Kahlua or other coffee flavored
    liqueur

½ cup cold water

4 eggs

3 oz semisweet chocolate

½ tsp cinnamon

⅛ tsp chili powder

¼ cup sugar

1 tsp butter

¼ cup almonds, slivered

1 ½ cups heavy cream

Sprinkle gelatin over ½ cup cold water in a measuring cup and let stand for about 5 minutes. Separate eggs, placing 2 egg whites in small bowl of an electric mixer and 4 egg yolks in top of a double boiler. Refrigerate remaining whites for use in another recipe. Let egg whites warm to room temperature.

Beat yolks slightly and stir in gelatin mixture, semisweet chocolate, cinnamon, chili powder, and 2 tablespoons of the sugar. Cook over hot (but not boiling) water, stirring for about 10 minutes, or until melted. Remove mixture from heat and stir in liqueur.

Pour chocolate mixture into a medium-sized bowl; place in a large bowl of ice water. Stir mixture occasionally until it cools and is the consistency of unbeaten egg whites, about 15 minutes. In a small skillet over medium heat, melt the butter. Add almonds and cook, stirring, just until golden brown (toasted). Cool.

In chilled bowl of an electric mixer, whip heavy cream until stiff; refrigerate. Meanwhile, with electric mixer, beat egg whites just until soft peaks form when beaters are slowly raised. Gradually beat in remaining 2 tablespoons sugar, beating until stiff peaks form when beaters are raised. With wire whisk or rubber spatula, using an under-and-over motion, fold beaten egg whites and 1 ½ cups whipped cream into the chocolate mixture. Cover and refrigerate remaining whipped cream. Turn filling into pie shell, spreading filling evenly. Refrigerate for about 3 hours, or until filling is firm.

Chop the toasted almonds. Spoon the remaining whipped cream into a pastry bag fitted with a #6 tip, and pipe whipped cream along inside edge of the pie crust. With a spoon, sprinkle almonds around the inside edge of the whipped cream. Refrigerate until ready to serve. Variation: Add ½ teaspoon cinnamon to chocolate mixture.

NOTE: Though it's rare for salmonella to grow in egg whites, it's not impossible. Consuming raw eggs may increase your risk of foodborne illness. Populations at particular risk include pregnant women, elderly, very young children, and individuals with compromised immune systems.

CHOCOLATE PEANUT BUTTER PIE

CRUST

Pastry for single crust 9-inch pie
1 cup peanuts, finely chopped

½ cup mini semi-sweet chocolate chips

FILLING

1 ¾ cup whipping cream
1 ¼ cup confectioner's sugar
1 Tbs vanilla extract

8 oz cream cheese, softened
½ cup creamy peanut butter
¼ cup milk

TOPPING

2 Tbs finely chopped peanuts

2 Tbs mini chocolate chips

Preheat oven to 450°F.

Line 9-inch pie plate with one crust. Gently press 1 cup peanuts into bottom and up sides of crust. Prick crust with fork. Bake at 450°F for 10 to 14 minutes or until light golden brown. Cool. Sprinkle with ½ cup miniature chocolate chips.

In medium bowl, beat whipping cream, ¼ cup confectioner's sugar, and vanilla until soft peaks form; set aside. In large bowl, beat cream cheese and peanut butter until light and fluffy. Add 1 cup confectioner's sugar and milk and beat until smooth and creamy. Fold in 1 ½ cups of the whipped cream. Spoon into cooled pie crust; spread evenly. Refrigerate at least 4 hours before serving. Garnish with remaining whipped cream and sprinkle with topping. Store in refrigerator.

ALMOND MACAROON CHERRY PIE

PIE

1 9-inch pie shell, unbaked
21 oz cherry pie filling
½ tsp cinnamon

⅛ tsp salt
1 tsp lemon juice

TOPPING

1 cup coconut
½ cup almonds, sliced
¼ cup sugar
⅛ tsp salt

¼ cup milk
1 Tbs butter, melted
¼ tsp almond extract
1 egg, beaten

Preheat oven to 400°F.

Roll out pie pastry and place in 9-inch pie pan.

In a large bowl, combine pie filling, cinnamon, salt, and lemon juice. Mix lightly. Spoon into the pie shell. Bake 20 minutes.

Meanwhile, combine all topping ingredients in a medium bowl and mix until blended. After pie has baked for 20 minutes, remove from oven, spread topping evenly over surface, and return pie to oven. Bake an additional 15 to 30 minutes, or until crust and topping are golden brown.

PEACH COBBLER WITH ALMOND STREUSEL

1 cup flour

¼ tsp salt

4 Tbs butter, chilled

⅔ cup brown sugar

½ tsp nutmeg

½ cup almonds; sliced

1 lemon

9 peaches; about 3 pounds, peeled and
    sliced

3 Tbs cornstarch

¼ tsp almond extract

2 Tbs dry bread crumbs

Heat oven to 475°F.

Grate 1 tsp of lemon zest from the lemon and squeeze 1 Tbs of juice. Add to peeled and sliced peaches along with the cornstarch. In a separate bowl, combine almonds, flour, salt, brown sugar, nutmeg, butter, and almond extract, using your fingers to work it into a crumbly mixture. Sprinkle breadcrumbs over bottom of pie shell and fill with peach mixture. Sprinkle almond crumb mixture on top. Bake 15 minutes. Reduce temperature to 350°F. Continue baking until top is browned and fruit juices are bubbling, 50 to 55 minutes. Cool completely before cutting.

RAISIN CRISSCROSS PIE

Pastry for two-crust 9-inch pie
1 cup brown sugar, packed
2 Tbs cornstarch
2 cups raisins
½ tsp orange peel, finely shredded

½ cup orange juice
½ tsp lemon peel, finely shredded
2 Tbs lemon juice
1 ⅓ cups cold water
½ cup walnuts, chopped

Preheat oven to 375°F.

In a saucepan, combine brown sugar and cornstarch. Stir in raisins, orange peel, orange juice, lemon peel, lemon juice, and water. Cook and stir over medium heat until thick and bubbly and then continue to cook and stir 1 minute more. Remove from heat, stir in walnuts. Fill a pastry-lined 9 inch pie plate with raisin mixture.

Roll out remaining pastry and cut into ½ inch wide strips. Weave strips on top of filling to make a lattice crust. Press ends of strips into rim of crust. Fold bottom pastry over the lattice strips, seal, and flute.

Cover edge of pie with foil. Bake for 20 minutes. Remove foil and bake about 20 more minutes or until crust is golden.

ALMOND-TOPPED PEAR PIE

1 9-inch pie shell, unbaked
3 Tbs cornstarch
¼ tsp ginger
⅛ tsp salt
½ cup dark corn syrup

2 Tbs butter
1 tsp lemon juice
½ tsp lemon rind, grated
4 medium pears, peeled and sliced

ALMOND TOPPING

1 cup flour
½ cup brown sugar, firmly packed
¼ tsp ginger, ground

½ cup butter
½ cup almonds, coarsely chopped

Preheat oven to 400°F.

Line a 9-inch pie plate with the unbaked pastry shell. Trim and flute edges. Chill.

Combine the cornstarch, ginger, and salt in a large bowl. Add the corn syrup, melted butter, lemon juice, and lemon rind, stirring until smooth. Add the pears and toss until well coated with the corn syrup mixture. Arrange the mixture in the unbaked pie shell.

To prepare the almond topping, combine the flour, brown sugar, and ginger in a bowl. Cut in the butter, using a pastry blender, until crumbly. Stir in the almonds. Sprinkle over the pears. Bake for 15 minutes, then reduce the heat to 350°F. and bake an additional 30 minutes, or until the topping and crust are golden brown. Cool on a wire rack.

APPLE BLUEBERRY CRUMBLE PIE

PASTRY

⅔ cup flour

⅓ cup butter, cubed

⅓ cup cream cheese, in pieces

1 Tbs sugar

FILLING

4 apples, cored, peeled, and sliced

1 ½ cups blueberries

½ cup sugar

⅓ cup flour

1 tsp cinnamon

1 Tbs breadcrumbs

CRUMBLE

1 cup flour

½ cup brown sugar, packed

½ cup butter, cubed

½ tsp cinnamon

Preheat oven to 400°F.

For pastry: Place flour, butter, cream cheese, and sugar in bowl of food processor and process 15 to 20 seconds or till dough forms soft ball on blade. Gather into a ball; flatten into disk, wrap, and chill until firm enough to roll. On lightly floured surface, roll out dough to 1/4-inch thickness. Line 9-inch pie plate with dough. Trim edges. Chill while preparing filling.

For filling: Toss apples and blueberries in a bowl with flour, sugar, and cinnamon until evenly coated. Sprinkle breadcrumbs over bottom of pie shell; fill with fruit mixture, mounded in center.

For crumble: Combine flour, brown sugar, butter, and cinnamon in food processor. Pat crumble mixture evenly over filling. Bake for about 45 minutes, or until apples are tender and juices are bubbling, shielding with foil if necessary.

AMISH APPLE PIE

1 unbaked 10-inch pie shell

STREUSEL

⅓ cup sugar
¼ cup brown sugar
10 Tbs flour

1 tsp cinnamon
1 tsp nutmeg
¼ tsp salt

PIE

½ cup butter, cold
½ cup walnuts, coarsely chopped
4 large apples
1 cup sugar
3 Tbs flour

½ tsp cinnamon
1 egg
1 cup heavy cream
1 tsp vanilla

In a food processor bowl, mix the first six ingredients for the streusel together. Add the butter and process until mixture is crumbly; it should still have a dry look, don't over-process. Add nuts, and set aside.

Preheat oven to 350°F.

Peel, core, and thinly slice the apples (should be about 4 cups). Place apples in pie shell. In a small bowl, mix the sugar, flour, and cinnamon. Beat the egg in a medium bowl, and add the cream and vanilla. Add the sugar mixture to the egg mixture, and blend. Pour over the apples.

Bake for 1 hour in the lower third of oven. After 20 minutes, sprinkle streusel over top, and continue baking about 40 minutes longer, or until the top puffs and is golden brown.

APPLE CREAM CHEESE PIE

1 9-inch pastry shell, unbaked
2 large apples, cored, peeled, and thinly
   sliced
¾ cup sugar
¼ tsp cinnamon, plus extra for dusting
¼ tsp nutmeg

½ cup walnuts, chopped
¼ tsp salt
2 eggs, beaten
½ cup heavy cream (or milk)
6 oz cream cheese
1 tsp vanilla extract

Preheat oven to 450°F.

Mix together the apple slices, ¼ cup of the sugar, cinnamon, and nutmeg. Arrange in the pastry shell. Sprinkle the nuts over the apples. Bake in a preheated oven for 15 minutes. Remove from the oven and turn the heat down to 325°F.

Cream together the remaining sugar, salt, and the cream cheese. Add the eggs and mix until smooth. Add to this the heavy cream and vanilla extract and mix well. Pour over the apples in the pie shell and bake in the 325°F oven for 40 minutes. When pie is cool, dust lightly with cinnamon.

APPLE KUTCHEN

3 cups flour, sifted
3 tsp baking powder
½ cup butter, softened

1 ½ cups sugar
1 egg
⅓ cup milk

TOPPING

½ cup butter, cold
½ cup brown sugar
½ cup granulated sugar
1 cup flour, sifted

1 tsp vanilla extract
Cinnamon, to taste
2 medium-sized apples

Preheat oven to 350°F.

Mix first six ingredients until soft dough forms. Pour into greased 9-inch pie plate. With buttered hands, spread batter to cover pie plate evenly. Core, peel, and slice apples and arrange to cover dough.

For the topping, mix remaining ingredients and crumble on top. Bake for 45 minutes.

Country Kitchen Tip

It's an old New England tradition to serve apple pie or other apple desserts with a slice of cheddar cheese. As an alternative, mix 1/2 cup shredded cheddar into the pie crust or topping!

APPLE PIE A LA APRICOT

1 9-inch pastry shell, uncooked
⅓ cup sugar
2 Tbs flour
1 cup milk
3 egg yolks
1 Tbs butter
½ tsp vanilla
5 to 7 tart cooking apples (cortland,
    Granny Smith, or macintosh are good
    options)

1 Tbs lemon juice
2 Tbs butter
2 Tbs sugar
¼ tsp nutmeg
¾ cup apricot preserves
1 egg yolk
1 Tbs water

Preheat oven to 425°F.

In small saucepan over medium heat, combine sugar and flour, mixing well. Stir in milk. Bring to a boil while stirring. Reduce heat and simmer until slightly thickened. In a bowl, beat 3 egg yolks slightly and add a small amount of hot mixture. Pour egg mixture into the saucepan.

Add 1 Tbs butter and vanilla. Cool. Peel and slice apples and sprinkle with lemon juice. In a skillet, combine 2 Tbs butter, sugar, and nutmeg, and melt. Add apples; sauté, stirring occasionally. Cook until almost tender, about 5 minutes. Remove from heat. Pour into pastry shell. Pour cooled filling over apples. In saucepan, heat preserves, 1 egg yolk, and water, and brush over pastry. Bake for 40 minutes or until golden.

APPLE CRUMBLE

Pastry for two 9-inch piecrusts, uncooked

CRUMB TOPPING

⅓ cup flour
⅓ cup dark brown sugar, packed
¼ tsp cinnamon

¼ tsp salt
¼ tsp ginger
2 Tbs cold, unsalted butter

FILLING

8 medium tart apples (Cortland, Granny
    Smith, or macintosh are good)
1 ½ tsp flour
¾ cup sugar
½ tsp cinnamon
½ tsp orange rind

½ tsp vanilla extract
⅛ tsp nutmeg
¼ tsp salt
½ cup honey
1 ½ Tbs unsalted butter
1 egg, beaten

For crumb topping: Mix flour, brown sugar, cinnamon, salt, and ginger. Work in butter with fingers until mixture is crumbly.

For filling: Peel, core, and cut apples into ½-inch slices. Put slices in large bowl; toss with 1 to 1 ½ Tbs flour. Add sugar, cinnamon, orange rind, vanilla extract, nutmeg, and salt. Stir in honey; let stand 1 hour.

Heat oven to 450°F.

Drain liquid from apples, reserve. Set ¼ cup of the crumb topping aside. Layer apples with remaining crumbs in pastry-lined pie plate. Use crumbs like mortar to build fruit up. Dot apples with 1 ½ Tbs butter. Sprinkle with 5 Tbs reserved apple liquid.

Roll out remaining dough; cut with knife or fluted pastry wheel into ½-inch-wide strips. Weave strips into lattice over fruit. Seal strips at edge of pan, moistening with apple liquid. Flute edge. Sprinkle reserved crumbs in holes of lattice. Brush only crust edge and strips with beaten egg.

Bake on foil-lined baking sheet for 5 minutes. Reduce oven temperature to 350°F; bake until apples are tender, 50 to 55 more minutes (or only 40 minutes if you like crunchier apples). Cool on wire rack to room temperature.

APPLE PIE WITH PORT AND CHEDDAR CHEESE CRUST

FILLING

1 ½ cup sugar
¼ cup cornstarch
⅔ cup apple juice
⅔ cup port

2 Tbs butter
1 lemon peel, grated
8 medium apples, cored, peeled, and
    sliced

CHEDDAR CHEESE CRUST

2 cups flour
1 tsp salt
⅓ cup butter

¾ cup sharp cheddar, shredded
5 Tbs cold water (or more)

Preheat oven to 375°F.

Combine sugar and cornstarch in large saucepan. Stir in apple juice, port, butter, and lemon peel. Cook over medium heat until mixture boils. Add apples and cook gently until barely tender.

To make cheddar cheese crust, mix flour, salt, and butter with pastry blender or in a food processor fitted with a blade until mixture resembles coarse meal. Stir in cheese. Add water gradually and mix lightly with fork to form dough. Divide pastry in halves and roll out one half to fit 9-inch pie pan. Roll second half of pastry and cut into 10 half-inch strips. Spoon filling into pastry-lined pan. Weave pastry strips across filling to make lattice top. Bake for 30 to 45 minutes, or until done. Serve warm.

APRICOT LATTICE PIE

1 cup sugar
⅛ tsp salt
¼ tsp nutmeg
¼ tsp cinnamon
2 ½ Tbs tapioca

Pastry for two-crust pie
3 cups fresh apricots, pitted
1 Tbs butter
Extra sugar for dusting

Preheat oven to 400°F.

In a small bowl mix the sugar, salt, spices, and tapioca. Sprinkle 1 tablespoon of mixture in unbaked pie shell. Fill with apricots. Cover with remaining sugar mixture. Dot with butter. Roll out remaining piecrust. Cut in half-inch strips with pastry wheel; arrange over fruit in lattice pattern. Sprinkle with sugar.

Bake for 15 minutes; reduce heat to 375°F and bake additional 30 minutes.

APPLE BROWN BETTY

2 cups cubed bread (no crusts)

2 Tbs butter, melted (for greasing)

4 large apples, cored, peeled, and thinly
    sliced apples

1 cup sugar

¼ tsp nutmeg

¼ tsp cinnamon

¼ tsp cloves

2 Tbs butter, cut into small pieces

1 lemon; grated rind and juice

Preheat oven to 375°F.

Place a layer of cubed bread in buttered soufflé dish that will hold 1½ quarts. Mix apples, sugar, and spices. Cover bread with a layer of apples. Dot with butter; add a little lemon juice and rind. Repeat layers, ending in bread cubes, until dish is well-heaped. Cover and bake for 30 minutes. Uncover and bake until apples are tender and crust golden brown, about 30 more minutes. Serve at once with vanilla ice cream. Like a soufflé, it will collapse if allowed to stand.

BAKEWELL RASPBERRY TART

¼ lb butter

1 9-inch pastry shell, baked and cooled

¼ cup almonds, ground

¼ cup caster sugar

2 large eggs

1 ½ cup raspberries or loganberries

Preheat the oven to 400°F. Dice the butter and barely melt it in a small saucepan over low heat. Away from the heat, add the sugar and then stir in the ground almonds (you can grind them in a food processor) and the lightly beaten eggs. Pour the berries into the pie shell, spreading them evenly, and then pour the almond mixture over the fruit. Bake for 35 to 40 minutes until the topping is pale gold and puffed up.

BANANA CREAM PIE

⅓ cup plus 3 tablespoons butter
35 vanilla wafers, crushed finely
½ cup sugar
¼ cup cornstarch

2 cups milk
3 large eggs, yolks only
1 tsp vanilla extract
3 medium-sized, firm, ripe bananas

TOPPING

1 ½ cups whipping cream
1 ½ Tbs sugar

½ tsp vanilla

By cooking the filling in the microwave, you eliminate the need for constant stirring and reduce the chance of scorching.

Lightly spray a 9-inch glass pie plate with vegetable cooking spray.

Crust: Cut the ⅓ cup butter in small pieces into a medium-size microwave-safe bowl. Microwave on high 15 to 18 seconds until soft but not melted. Add cookie crumbs and stir with a fork until blended. Press firmly and evenly over bottom and up sides of prepared pie plate. Microwave on medium 2 to 2 ½ minutes, rotating dish a half turn once, until crust is set.

Let cool before filling.

Filling: Mix sugar and cornstarch in a 2-quart, microwave-safe bowl. Gradually whisk in milk, then egg yolks until well blended. Microwave uncovered on high 4 ½ to 5 ½ minutes, stirring once, until mixture starts to rise around edges. Continue cooking on high 1 to 1 ½ minutes, stirring once, until filling starts to thicken. Whisk in remaining 3 tablespoons butter and the vanilla extract until custard has a pudding consistency. Place plastic wrap directly on custard to prevent skin from forming. Refrigerate 1 hour or until cool.

To assemble: peel bananas, quarter lengthwise, and cut crosswise on half-inch pieces. Mix with 1 cup of the cooled custard. Spread over bottom of crust. Spread remaining custard on top. Refrigerate 3 hours or up to 1 day (bananas will darken slightly).

Topping: beat cream until slightly thickened. Beat in sugar and vanilla and beat until stiff peaks form when beaters are lifted.

Spread pie with whipped cream. Refrigerate until serving time.

DEEP-DISH RHUBARB-STRAWBERRY PIE

Pastry for 9-inch piecrust

¾ cup sugar

⅓ cup flour, sifted

1 tsp cinnamon

½ tsp cloves

1 lb fresh rhubarb

1 pint strawberries

2 Tbs butter

Milk or cream

Sugar

Preheat oven to 425°F.

Mix sugar, flour, cinnamon, and cloves in a bowl.

Wash rhubarb, trim ends, and cut into 1-inch pieces (you should have about 6 cups).

Wash strawberries, hull, and halve (you should have about 4 cups). Place both in a large bowl. Sprinkle with sugar mixture; toss lightly to mix. Let stand 15 minutes. Toss again.

Spoon rhubarb-strawberry filling into an 8 x 8 x 2-inch baking dish; dot with butter or margarine.

Prepare pastry: Roll out to a 10-inch square on a lightly floured surface. Cut in half-inch strips with a pastry wheel or knife. Weave strips into a lattice. Cover filling. Turn ends under just enough so that strips touch sides of baking dish. Brush lattice top with milk or cream; sprinkle with sugar.

Bake for 40 minutes, or until pastry is golden and juices bubble up. Cool. Serve warm with whipped cream, if desired.

SOUR CREAM PEACH PIE

Pastry for 9-inch pie

⅓ cup flour

½ cup sugar

1 cup sour cream

5 cups peaches, peeled and quartered

¼ cup brown sugar, lightly packed

Preheat oven to 450°F.

Line 9-inch pie plate with pastry. Trim and flute edges; do *not* prick pastry. Combine flour, sugar, and sour cream (use commercial sour cream from store). Arrange flat edge of peach quarters on pastry in concentric circles. Pour sour cream on top. Bake 15 minutes at 450°F, then lower heat to 350°F and bake 25 to 30 minutes, or until filling is set. Sprinkle brown sugar over hot pie. Broil 1 to 2 minutes until sugar is melted. Serve warm.

CRANBERRY PEAR TART

¼ cup water
¾ cup sugar
½ cup red currant jelly
3 cup fresh or frozen cranberries
    (thawed, if frozen)
1 firm, ripe pear, pared, cored, and
    chopped (about 1 cup)
½ cup butter

1 ¼ cups flour
¼ cup sugar
⅔ cup finely chopped walnuts
½ tsp cinnamon
2 egg yolks
½ tsp cream of tartar
4 egg whites
½ cup sugar

Preheat oven to 375°F.

Combine the water, ¾ cup sugar, and the jelly in a medium-size saucepan. Place over medium heat until the jelly melts and the sugar dissolves. Bring to a boil. Add the cranberries and the pear. Cook, uncovered, over medium heat until the cranberries pop and the mixture thickens slightly, for 10 to 15 minutes. Cool completely.

Cut the butter into the flour in a medium-size bowl with a pastry blender, until crumbly. Mix together the ¼ cup sugar, walnuts, and cinnamon. Add the egg yolks. Mix lightly with a fork just until the pastry holds together and cleans the side of the bowl. Press the dough over the bottom and up the sides of a 9-inch tart pan with a removable bottom. Prick the bottom with a fork. Refrigerate for 30 minutes.

Bake the shell for 12 to 15 minutes, or until golden brown. Cool completely. Spoon the cooled cranberry filling into the cooled pastry shell. Reset the oven to 400°F.

Beat the egg whites with the cream of tartar in a medium-size bowl until soft peaks form. Gradually beat in the ½ cup sugar until stiff peaks form. Spread half the meringue over top of the tart. Pipe the remaining meringue in a lattice pattern.

Bake for 3 to 6 minutes, or until the meringue is golden brown. Decorate with additional cranberries, if desired.

BLACKBERRY COBBLER

1 stick unsalted butter
1 cup water
1 cup plus 2 Tbs sugar
1 ¼ cups flour

1 tsp baking powder
⅓ cup milk
½ tsp cinnamon
3 cups blackberries, fresh or thawed

Preheat oven to 350°F.

In a 10-inch pie or baking dish melt half stick of butter. Keep remaining half stick chilled.

Heat water and 1 cup sugar until sugar it is dissolved.

In a food processor, pulse together flour, baking powder, and remaining half stick of chilled butter cut up into small pieces until mixture resembles fine meal. Add milk and pulse just until dough forms. Turn dough on to lightly floured surface, and with floured rolling pin roll out to an eleven 11 x 9 rectangle.

Sprinkle dough with cinnamon, then sprinkle blackberries evenly over it. Beginning with a long side, roll up dough jelly-roll fashion and cut into 1 ½-inch slices. (Slices will come apart and be messy.) Arrange slices, cut side up, on butter in baking dish; pour sugar syrup over slices, soaking dough, and bake in the middle of the oven for 45 minutes. Sprinkle remaining 2 Tbs. sugar over top and bake an additional 15 minutes or until nicely browned.

Serve hot with vanilla ice cream or whipped cream.

CHERRY PIE

Pastry for 2 9-inch piecrusts
4 cups pitted, fresh red cherries
1 Tbs lemon juice
1 ¼ cups sugar
¼ cup flour

⅛ tsp salt
⅛ tsp cloves
¼ tsp cinnamon
1 Tbs butter

Preheat oven to 400°F.

Line a 9-inch pie pan with pastry; refrigerate until ready to use. In large bowl, sprinkle cherries with lemon juice. Mix sugar, flour, salt, and spices; add to cherries and mix gently but thoroughly. Pour into unbaked pastry crust; dot with butter. Put on top crust; seal and crimp edges; cut slits to let steam escape. Bake for 35 to 40 minutes, or until nicely browned. Cool.

ALMOND PUMPKIN PIE

1 9-in unbaked pastry shell
16 oz pumpkin (2 cups)
14 oz sweetened condensed milk
2 eggs
1 tsp almond extract

½ tsp ground cinnamon
6 oz toffee chips
1 cup almonds, toasted and finely
    chopped

Preheat oven to 425°F.

In a large mixing bowl, combine all ingredients except pastry shell, toffee chips, and almonds. Mix well. Stir in half of toffee chips and almonds. Pour into pastry shell. Top with remaining toffee chips and almonds. Bake 15 minutes. Reduce oven temperature to 350°F and bake 30 minutes longer, or until knife inserted near center comes out clean. Cool.

Refrigerate leftovers.

AMISH CUSTARD PIE

1 9-inch pie shell, unbaked
⅓ cup sugar
2 tsp flour
½ tsp salt

3 eggs
3 cups milk
¼ tsp nutmeg

Preheat oven to 350°F.

Combine sugar, flour, salt, and eggs and mix until smooth. Heat milk to boiling point. Add 1 cup hot milk to egg mixture. Pour that into the remaining hot milk.

Pour into unbaked pie shell. Sprinkle nutmeg over top. Bake for 45 to 60 minutes.

SHOO FLY PIE

½ cup molasses
1 egg yolk
½ tsp baking soda
¾ cup boiling water
¾ cup flour
½ cup brown sugar
2 Tbs butter

⅛ tsp nutmeg
⅛ tsp ginger
⅛ tsp cloves
½ tsp cinnamon
¼ tsp salt
1 pastry for 9-inch pie

Preheat oven to 450°F.

Line 9-inch pie plate with pastry. Mix molasses and egg yolk. Dissolve baking soda in boiling water and add to egg and molasses. Set aside. Stir dry ingredients together, mixing well. Cut in butter until mixture looks like coarse crumbs. Pour molasses mixture into pie shell. Sprinkle crumbs evenly over top. Do not stir. Bake for 15 minutes, then reduce heat to 350°F and bake 20 minutes longer. Cool and serve.

OATMEAL PIE

1 9-inch pie shell, unbaked

1 cup sugar

3 Tbs flour

1 tsp cinnamon

¼ tsp salt

4 eggs

1 ½ Tbs butter, melted

1 cup light corn syrup

1 tsp grated orange rind

1 tsp vanilla extract

1 cup quick oats

Preheat oven to 350°F.

Mix sugar, flour, cinnamon, and salt. Beat eggs until frothy. Add dry mixture to eggs. Add corn syrup, melted butter, orange rind, vanilla extract, and quick oats. Mix well. Pour into shell. Bake for 45 minutes.

SUGAR PIE

1 9-inch pie shell, unbaked
1 cup brown sugar
3 Tbs flour
¼ tsp salt

1 ½ cup evaporated milk
3 Tbs butter
Cinnamon to taste

Preheat oven to 350°F.

In a small bowl, blend together the sugar, flour, and salt. Spread in bottom of pie shell. Pour the milk over the sugar mixture, but do not stir. Dot with the butter and sprinkle cinnamon over all. Bake for 50 to 60 minutes, or until filling bubbles in center. This will not be a firm custard, so don't worry if it doesn't look like the custard pies you are accustomed to! Serve at room temperature and refrigerate leftovers.

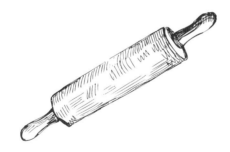

CHOCOLATE CUSTARD PIE

1 9-inch pie crust, unbaked
1 ⅓ sticks butter
1 ½ squares unsweetened baking choco-
    late

1 ⅓ cup sugar
3 small eggs
⅓ tsp salt
1 tsp vanilla extract

Preheat oven to 375°F.

Melt butter and chocolate over boiling water. Mix sugar, eggs, salt, and vanilla; add to chocolate mixture. Pour into pie shell and bake for about 35 minutes.

CITRUS CHIFFON PIE

1 9-inch pastry shell, baked
1 envelope unflavored gelatin
½ cup sugar
Dash of salt
4 egg yolks
½ cup lemon juice

½ cup orange juice
¼ cup water
½ tsp lemon peel, grated
½ tsp orange peel, grated
4 egg whites
⅓ cup sugar

Thoroughly mix gelatin, ½ cup sugar, and salt in saucepan. Beat together egg yolks, fruit juices, and water; stir into gelatin mixture. Cook and stir over medium heat just until mixture comes to boiling. Remove from heat; stir in peels. Chill, stirring occasionally, until mixture mounds slightly when dropped from a spoon. Beat egg whites till soft peaks form. Gradually add ⅓ cup sugar, beating to stiff peaks; fold in gelatin mixture. Pile into cooled baked pastry shell. Chill until firm.

Trim with whipped cream and thin orange slices cut in fourths.

COCONUT CREAM PIE

1 9-inch pie crust, baked and cooled
1 cup coconut
4 egg whites, at room temperature
¼ tsp cream of tartar

¼ tsp vanilla extract
8 Tbs sugar
2 Tbs coconut for top of meringue,
    toasted

PASTRY CREAM

8 egg yolks
1 cup sugar
1 quart milk

½ cup cornstarch
1 ½ teaspoon vanilla extract

Preheat oven to 350°F.

For pastry cream: Whisk egg yolks and sugar together until thick. Dissolve cornstarch in 1 cup cold milk. Beat into egg yolks. In a large saucepan, bring remaining 3 cups milk to a full rolling boil. Remove from heat and gradually whisk in egg yolk mixture. Return to heat and cook, stirring constantly with a whisk or wooden spoon, until mixture thickens. Remove from heat, beat in vanilla extract, and strain into a clean bowl if necessary. Cover surface of pastry cream directly with plastic wrap and refrigerate.

While the pastry cream is still hot, stir in coconut. Pour into pie crust. Beat egg whites, cream of tartar, and vanilla extract until they form soft peaks. Gradually add sugar and beat until peaks are stiff and egg whites are shiny but not dry. Spread meringue over hot filling, sealing to edge of pie crust. Sprinkle with coconut. Bake until meringue is golden, 12 to 15 minutes. Cool before slicing. Refrigerate leftovers.

CREAM CHEESE RHUBARB PIE

¼ cup cornstarch

1 cup sugar

⅛ tsp salt

½ cup water

3 cups sliced fresh or frozen rhubarb
 (cut in half-inch pieces)

1 9-inch pastry shell, unbaked

TOPPING

1 package (8 oz) cream cheese

Whipped cream

Sliced almonds

Preheat oven to 425°F.

In a saucepan, combine the cornstarch, sugar, and salt. Add water and stir until well combined. Add rhubarb. Cook, stirring often until mixture boils and thickens. Pour into pie shell. Bake for 10 minutes. Meanwhile for topping, beat cream cheese, eggs, and sugar until smooth. Pour over pie. Return to oven. Reduce heat to 325°F. Bake for 35 minutes or until set. Cool.

Chill several hours or overnight. Garnish with whipped cream and almonds.

GRASSHOPPER PIE

1 cup chocolate wafer crumbs
3 Tbs melted butter
2 Tbs milk
2 Tbs white creme de cacao
1 pt vanilla ice cream

¼ cup sugar
1 cup heavy cream
3 ¼ cup miniature marshmallows
¼ cup green creme de menthe

GARNISH

Whipped cream
Chocolate curls

Marshmallows
Strawberries

Combine wafer crumbs, sugar, and butter in a medium bowl. Press mixture along sides and bottom of a 9-inch pie plate; chill. Whip 1 cup heavy cream; chill. In top of double boiler, combine milk and marshmallows. Heat over boiling water, stirring until marshmallows are melted. Remove from heat; cool completely, stirring occasionally. Add creme de cacao and creme de menthe and fold mixture into whipped cream. Spread slightly softened ice cream on pie crust to form an even layer. Pour marsh-mallow mixture over ice cream; freeze for 6 hours or overnight. If desired, garnish with whipped cream, chocolate curls, marshmallows, strawberries. May be made several days in advance.

FRENCH SILK PIE

Pastry for two-crust 9-inch pie
¼ lb butter
¾ cup sugar
1 tsp vanilla extract

1 oz melted chocolate
2 large eggs
Whipped cream
Chocolate shavings

Combine the butter and sugar and mix until creamy and fluffy. Add the vanilla extract and chocolate. Mix well. Add one egg and beat with a mixer for 5 minutes. Add another egg and beat for an additional 5 minutes. Pour into a baked pie shell. Refrigerate overnight. Top with whipped cream and shaved chocolate.

HONEY CHEESE PIE WITH STRAWBERRY COMPOTE

CRUST

¼ cup (½ stick) unsalted butter
2 Tbs honey
35 vanilla wafer cookies

¾ cup whole almonds
¾ cup walnuts
¼ tsp salt

FILLING

2 8-oz packages cream cheese,
   room temperature
1 15- to 16-oz container whole milk
   ricotta cheese
½ cup plus 1 tablespoon sugar

½ cup plus 1 tablespoon honey
4 extra-large eggs
2 tsp vanilla extract
½ tsp lemon extract

COMPOTE

3 cups small strawberries, hulled and
   quartered

⅓ cup honey

GARNISH

Strawberry blossoms, violets, or other
   small edible flowers (optional)

Additional honey

For Crust: Preheat oven to 350°F. Wrap a spring-form pan of 10-inch diameter by 2 ½-inch height with foil. Bring butter and honey to a boil in a small, heavy saucepan, stirring occasionally. Remove from heat. Finely grind vanilla wafers in processor. Add nuts and salt to processor. Add butter mixture and process until nuts are finely chopped. Press mixture onto bottom and 1 inch up sides of prepared pan. Bake crust until golden, about 12 minutes. Transfer to rack and cool. Reduce oven temperature to 325°F.

For Filling: Beat together cream cheese and ricotta cheese in a large bowl until smooth. Mix in sugar and honey. Add eggs, one at a time, beating well after each addition. Mix in vanilla and lemon extracts. Pour filling into crust.

Bake pie for about 1 hour 10 minutes, or until puffed, golden, and center moves only slightly when pan is gently shaken. Transfer to rack and cool completely. (Can be prepared 1 day ahead. Cover and chill.)

For Compote: Mix quartered strawberries and honey in large bowl. (Can be made 4 hours ahead. Cover; chill.)

Run small, sharp knife around sides of pan to loosen pie. Release pan sides. Drizzle additional honey over pie in zigzag pattern. Transfer pie to serving platter. Using a slotted spoon, transfer some of strawberry compote to top of pie, if desired. Garnish pie with strawberry blossoms, if desired. Cut pie into wedges and serve with remaining strawberry compote.

LEMON MERINGUE PIE

Pastry for single-crust 9-inch pie

LEMON FILLING

¼ tsp cornstarch
3 Tbs flour
1 ¾ cup sugar
¼ tsp salt
2 cups water

4 egg yolks, lightly beaten
½ cup lemon juice
1 Tbs grated lemon peel
1 Tbs butter

MERINGUE

4 egg whites
¼ tsp cream of tarter

½ cup sugar

Preheat oven to 450°F.

Line a 9-inch pie plate with pastry and prick entire surface evenly with fork. Bake 8 to 10 minutes, or until golden-brown. Cool on rack.

In medium saucepan, combine cornstarch, flour, 1 ¾ cups sugar, and salt, mixing well. Gradually add 2 cups water, stirring until smooth. Over medium heat, bring to boiling, stirring occasionally; boil 1 minute, until shiny and translucent. Quickly stir some of hot mixture into yolks. Pour back into hot mixture; stir to blend. Return to heat; cook over low heat 5 minutes, stirring occasionally. Remove from heat; stir in lemon juice, lemon peel and butter. Pour into pie shell. Reduce oven to 400°F.

In medium bowl, with mixer at medium speed, beat whites with cream of tartar until frothy. Gradually beat in sugar, 2 Tbs. at a time, beating after each addition. Beat at high speed until stiff peaks form when beater is slowly raised. Spread meringue over lemon filling, carefully sealing to edge of the crust and swirling the top decoratively. Bake 7 to 9 minutes, or until the meringue is golden-brown. Let cool completely on rack 2 ½ to 3 hours. Cut with wet knife.

MAPLE CREAM PIE

Pastry for single crust 9-inch pie,   ⅔ cup maple syrup
   pre-baked   Pinch of salt
1 can sweetened condensed milk   Whipped cream

Combine sweetened condensed milk, syrup, and salt in saucepan. Stir constantly over very low heat until bubbles form in center. Cool slightly. Pour into precooked shell. Top with whipped cream when ready to serve.

MARY BERGIN'S BROWNED BUTTER TOFFEE TART

PATE SUCREE (SWEET PASTRY CRUST)

1 ¼ cup All-purpose flour

2 Tbs sugar

½ cup (1 stick) cold butter, cut in pieces

1 egg yolk

2 Tbs water

FILLING

2 eggs

¾ cup sugar

6 Tbs flour

½ cup (1 stick) butter

1 ½ tsp vanilla extract

¾ cup chocolate covered toffee, chopped

For pate sucree: Place flour, sugar, and butter in food processor fitted with steel blade. Process until mixture resembles fine meal. In a small bowl, whisk together egg yolk and water. Add to butter mixture. Process until dough just holds together. If dough appears dry, add a little more water. (To mix by hand, combine dry ingredients in medium bowl. Using a pastry blender or two table knives, cut in butter until mixture resembles coarse meal. Add liquid ingredients with fork and stir until dough leaves sides of bowl.) Flatten dough into a circle. Wrap in plastic wrap. Refrigerate 1 hour. On lightly floured board, roll out pastry to an 11-inch circle. Transfer dough to a 9- or 9 ½-inch tart pan. Trim edges and refrigerate 30 minutes.

For filling: Heat oven to 350°F. In a medium mixing bowl, whisk together eggs and sugar, then whisk into flour. In a 10-inch skillet, heat the butter over medium heat. Continue cooking until butter has turned a golden brown color, stirring occasionally. Be careful that butter does not burn. Whisk butter and vanilla extract into egg mixture until smooth. Place tart shell on baking sheet. Pour in filling and spread evenly. Sprinkle with chopped toffee. Bake until top is deep golden brown and firm to touch, 30 minutes. Cool on wire rack.

Serve slightly warm or at room temperature.

MISSISSIPPI MIST PIE

CRUST

2 cups vanilla wafer crumbs (about 50 wafers)

5 Tbs butter, melted

FILLING

2 pt fresh strawberries
8-oz package light cream cheese, softened
1 14-oz can sweetened condensed milk

½ cup fresh lime juice (about 6 to 8 limes)
1 Tbs green creme de menthe liqueur

TOPPING

1 cup whipping cream
3 Tbs sugar

½ tsp vanilla
Lime slice, for garnish

Combine crumbs and butter in a small bowl. Press firmly on bottom and up side of a 9-inch pie plate. Refrigerate until firm.

Reserving 3 strawberries for garnish, cut off stem ends of remaining berries so they are no more than 1 inch tall. Arrange on crust, cut ends down, and refrigerate. Beat cream cheese until smooth. Add sweetened condensed milk; beat well. Add lime juice and liqueur and continue beating until thoroughly combined. Pour into prepared crust, covering strawberries. Refrigerate at least one hour.

Whip cream until soft peaks form. Gradually add sugar and vanilla and whip until stiff and glossy. Using a pastry bag with a decorating tip, pipe a lattice design on top of the pie. Garnish with the reserved strawberries and lime slice.

PEACH SKILLET PIE

Pastry for 9-inch pie
6 fresh peaches, peeled
½ cup sugar

½ tsp salt
¼ tsp cinnamon
1 ½ Tbs butter

Preheat oven to 425°F.

Roll out pastry dough on a lightly floured board until large enough to line an 8-inch skillet or frying pan, allowing dough to hang over edge. Slice skinned peaches into pastry-lined pan. Sprinkle with sugar, salt, and cinnamon. Dot with butter. Fold the dough over the edge toward center, leaving a small space uncovered. Bake until fruit is bubbly and crust is browned, about 25 to 30 minutes.

PEPPERMINT STICK PIE

CRUST

1 ½ cups chocolate wafer crumbs   ¼ cup butter, melted

FILLING

24 large marshmallows   6 drops peppermint extract
½ cup milk   6 drops red food color
1 tsp vanilla   1 cup whipping cream
⅛ tsp salt   2 Tbs peppermint candy, crushed

Heat oven to 350°F.

Mix wafer crumbs and melted butter. Press firmly against bottom and sides of an ungreased 9-inch pie plate. Bake 10 minutes. Cool. Heat marshmallows and milk over low heat, stirring constantly, just until marshmallows are melted. Remove from heat; stir in vanilla, salt, peppermint extract, and food color. Refrigerate, stirring occasionally, until mixture mounds slightly when dropped from a spoon.

Beat whipping cream in chilled bowl until stiff. Stir marshmallow mix until blended well; fold into whipped cream. Pour into crust. Refrigerate at least 12 hours. Before serving, sprinkle with crushed candy.

TARTE AU SUCRE JAUNE (BROWN SUGAR PIE)

Pastry for single crust 9-inch pie
1 cup brown sugar
1 Tbs flour

1 Tbs butter
4 Tbs heavy cream

Preheat oven to 400°F.

Line nine-inch pie plate with rolled-out pastry. Mix the brown sugar, flour, butter, and heavy cream. Pour the mixture into an uncooked pie crust and bake for about 30 minutes.

FLAKY PIE CRUST

Yields 2 9-inch pie crusts

3 cups unbleached all-purpose flour

1 tsp salt

1 ⅓ cups vegetable shortening; OR

1 cup lard

1 large egg

1 Tbs vinegar

5 Tbs cold water

Cut the shortening into the flour and salt. Beat the egg, vinegar, and water together. Add 1 Tbs. of the water mixture over part of the flour mixture. Gently toss with a fork. Push to one side of the bowl. Sprinkle the next tablespoon of the water mixture onto the dry part, toss lightly, and push to the side of the bowl. Repeat until all of the water mixture is gone and all of the flour mixture is moistened. Gather with your fingers and form into a ball. Divide into three equal portions. Form each into a ball and flatten slightly. Roll to a ⅛-inch thickness on a lightly floured surface. If the edges split, push them together to seal. Always roll from the center to the edge, using light strokes.

Country Kitchen Tip

For a pre-baked piecrust, prick the crust with a fork, line with aluminum foil, and fill with pie weights, or a thin layer of uncooked rice or dried beans. Bake in a preheated 450°F. oven for about 20 minutes, or until lightly browned.

WHOLE WHEAT PIE CRUST

Yields 1 9-inch pie crust.

1 ½ cups whole wheat pastry flour   ½ cup butter, cold
2 tsp sugar   4 to 5 Tbs cold milk
½ tsp salt

Combine flour, sugar, and salt in a food processor fitted with a steel blade and pulse to mix. Cut butter into half-inch pieces, add to flour mixture, and pulse until mixture forms a coarse meal. Add cold milk a little at a time, pulsing until dough begins to hold together.

ALL BUTTER PIE CRUST

Yields 1 nine-inch pie crust

1 ¼ cups all-purpose flour
½ cup unsalted butter, cold

½ tsp salt
3 to 4 Tbs ice water.

Combine flour and salt in a food processor fitted with a steel blade and pulse to mix. Cut butter into half-inch pieces, add to flour mixture, and pulse until mixture forms a coarse meal. Add ice water a little at a time, pulsing until dough begins to hold together.

GLUTEN-FREE PIE CRUST

Yields 1 nine-inch pie crust

1 cup white rice flour	1 tsp salt
¼ cup potato starch (not potato flour)	2 Tbs sugar
¼ cup tapioca starch	½ cup butter, cold
1 teaspoon xanthan gum	2 to 4 tablespoons ice water

Combine all dry ingredients in a food processor fitted with a steel blade and pulse to mix. Cut butter into half-inch pieces, add to flour mixture, and pulse until mixture forms a coarse meal. Add ice water a little at a time, pulsing until dough begins to hold together.

Remove the dough from the food processor and form into a ball. Flatten it slightly, wrap in plastic wrap, and refrigerate for at least one hour. Remove from refrigerator a few minutes before ready to use. Roll the dough between two pieces of waxed paper sprinkled with gluten-free flour.

FLAKY COTTAGE CHEESE PASTRY

Yields 1 nine-inch pie crust

2 cups all-purpose flour   1 cup cottage cheese
1 cup butter, cut into ½-inch slices

Measure the flour into a bowl and cut in the butter until it resembles very coarse crumbs. Stir in the cottage cheese and blend with a fork until a dough forms. Knead just until the dough is blended, 5 to 10 strokes. Cover and Chill for 30 minutes, or until ready to use before rolling.

GRAHAM CRACKER PIE SHELL

Yields 1 nine-inch pie crust

7 large graham crackers   3 Tbs butter, melted

Break graham crackers into small pieces and place in a gallon-size, resealable plastic bag. Press with a rolling pin or a large jar to make crumbs. Continue until all crumbs are fine (total of 1 ¼ cups). Empty into bowl. Melt the butter, add to crumbs, and mix well with a fork. Set aside 2 Tbs. to use later as the garnish on the pie filling. Using the back of a spoon, press remainder of crumb mixture evenly on bottom and sides of a 9-inch pie plate. Chill in refrigerator for 3 hours or longer before filling.

Cakes and Cupcakes

SOUR CREAM BLUEBERRY GINGERBREAD

1 cup molasses
1 cup sour cream
2 cups all-purpose flour
½ tsp salt
1 tsp ginger

2 tsp baking soda
1 cup blueberries
1 medium apple, cored, peeled, and
    chopped (optional)

Preheat oven to 375°F.

Mix together the molasses and sour cream. Separately mix together the dry ingredients, but reserve one-fourth cup of the flour to mix with the blueberries. Add the dry ingredients to the molasses mixture. Fold in the blueberries (and apple, if desired), and place in the oven right away. Bake in a greased 9 x 9 baking pan for 35 to 40 minutes or until the top springs back when touched and the edges have pulled away from the pan. The gingerbread should be about 1 ½ inches thick.

APPLE JOHNNY-CAKE

1 cup cornmeal
1 Tbs sugar
½ tsp salt
1 Tbs butter, softened

¾ cup boiling water
3 Tbs milk
1 cup chopped apple

Preheat oven to 375°F.

Mix the cornmeal, sugar, salt, and butter together. Scald with the boiling water, until the mixture is a little thicker than will spread; add the milk and chopped apple. Spread on well-greased pans to a thickness of one-fourth inch, crease in squares with the back of a knife, and bake for 25 to 30 minutes or until golden brown. Split and serve warm with butter.

CHOCOLATE NUGGET CAKE

2 cups light brown sugar
½ cup butter, softened
1 cup buttermilk
2 cups all-purpose flour
½ tsp salt

½ tsp baking soda
1 tsp baking powder
1 cup raisins or chopped dates
1 cup walnut or pecan meats
2 squares chocolate (16 oz), melted

Preheat oven to 350°F.

Cream the butter and the sugar. Sift the salt, baking powder, and baking soda with the flour. Mix the flour and milk with the shortening and sugar mixture, alternating between the two additions. Add the nuts, raisins, and, lastly, the melted chocolate. Bake in a greased and floured 9 x 13 pan for 35 minutes, or until a toothpick inserted into the center comes out clean. Dust with powdered sugar or frost with mocha icing.

LIGHT FRUIT CAKE

2 cups butter
2 cups sugar
4 cups pastry flour
8 eggs
1 cup plus 3 Tbs brandy*

1 lb candied pineapple
1 lb candied cherries
1 lb blanched almonds
½ pound citron
2 cups shredded coconut

Shred the cherries, cut the pineapple and citron in bits, and chop the almonds. Add three tablespoons of brandy to the fruit and nut mix and allow to stand overnight.

Preheat oven to 275°F. Cream the butter and the sugar together, add the egg yolks well beaten, then the coconut, flour, one cup of brandy, and the egg whites (whipped stiff), putting them in alternately. Finally stir in the fruit and nuts.

Grease and line 9-inch round pans with 2 layers of parchment paper, then grease again. Pour batter into pans and bake for 2 hours, or until toothpick inserted into the center comes out clean.

*Apple cider or white grape juice can be substituted for the brandy, if desired.

ORANGE CHOCOLATE CAKE

¼ lb bitter chocolate
½ cup butter, softened
1 ½ cups sugar
1 ½ cups milk
2 cups pastry flour
2 eggs, well beaten

2 tsp vanilla extract
1 tsp baking soda
¾ tsp salt
2 Tbsp orange zest
3 Tbs hot water

Preheat oven to 375° F.

Coarsely chop the chocolate and put in a saucepan with the milk and ½ cup sugar, letting it heat to boiling point, stirring occasionally, and boiling five minutes. Cool and add the vanilla extract. In the meantime, cream the butter and the remaining sugar thoroughly together, add the beaten eggs, and stir vigorously. Add the hot water. Sift together the flour, baking soda, salt, and orange zest and add alternately with the chocolate mixture to the dry ingredients, stirring them in thoroughly. Bake in two 9-inch greased pans for 30 minutes.

Allow cakes to cool while making Orange Icing (page 180). Frost cake and garnish with melted, swirled chocolate, chocolate shavings, candied orange peel, miniature chocolate chips, and/or mint sprigs.

HONEY NUT GINGERBREAD

1 cup honey
⅓ cup butter or margarine
1 cup cold water
2 cups whole wheat flour
1 cup chopped nuts
2 eggs

2 tsp baking powder
1 tsp ginger
1 tsp cinnamon
¼ tsp baking soda
½ tsp salt

Preheat oven to 350°F.

Cream the butter and honey together. Add the eggs, well-beaten. Mix and sift the dry ingredients together, and add alternately with the water. Add the chopped nuts last. Bake in a greased 9 x 9 pan for 45 minutes, or until a toothpick inserted into the center comes out clean.

MAPLE LAYER CAKE

3 eggs
1 cup soft maple sugar (or 1 cup brown
    sugar with ¼ cup real maple syrup)
1 cup pastry flour, sifted

½ tsp salt
1 tsp baking powder
1 cup whipping cream
¼ cup grated maple sugar

Preheat oven to 320°F.

Beat the egg yolks until light and fluffy. Add the maple sugar and the flour with the salt and baking powder. In a separate bowl, beat the egg whites until stiff. Fold the egg whites into the mixture. Mix quickly and bake for 30 minutes in two greased and floured layer-cake pans (use one 8-inch round pan and one 10-inch round pan for the layered effect shown here).

Whip the cream with the grated maple sugar. Spread cream between the two layers and on top and decorate with fruit, or ice with maple fondant (page 178), or merely sprinkle with powdered sugar.

MOTHER'S GINGERBREAD

1 cup brown sugar
½ cup margarine
½ cup heavy cream
2 eggs
1 cup molasses

2 ½ cups all-purpose flour
½ tsp baking soda
1 Tbs ginger
½ tsp salt
½ cup milk

Preheat oven to 350°F.

Cream the margarine and sugar together. Beat the eggs well. Add the heavy cream and eggs, then the molasses. Sift the dry ingredients together and add them to the other mixture, alternating with the milk. Pour into an 8-inch square baking pan, well-greased and floured. Bake for 45 minutes, or until a toothpick inserted into the center comes out clean.

AUNT REBECCA'S OLD-FASHIONED SPONGE CAKE

1 ⅓ cups powdered sugar
1 cup all-purpose flour
½ lemon, juice and rind

5 eggs
Pinch of salt

Preheat oven to 325°F.

Separate eggs and beat yolks with sugar until light and creamy, at least ten minutes. Add lemon juice and rind. Beat egg whites stiff, fold into mixture, and then sift in the flour and salt slowly, stirring gently. Bake in a greased 9-inch tube pan for 50 minutes, or until the center springs back when touched.

COCOA APPLESAUCE CAKE

1 cup sugar
½ cup sour cream
1 cup hot applesauce
1 ¼ tsp baking soda
1 Tbs baking cocoa

1 tsp cinnamon
½ tsp cloves
2 cups all-purpose flour
1 cup raisins

Preheat oven to 350°F.

Mix together cocoa, spices, flour, baking soda, and raisins. In a separate bowl, put the sugar, sour cream, and hot applesauce. Beat in the flour mixture. Bake in a well-greased loaf pan for 45 minutes, or until a toothpick inserted into the center comes out clean. Serve plain or frost with Sour Cream Icing (page 178).

WHITE LAYER CAKE

1 ½ cup granulated sugar
½ cup butter
1 cup milk
3 cups cake flour

4 tsp baking powder
1 tsp vanilla extract
6 egg whites

Preheat oven to 350°F.

Cream the butter, add sugar gradually, and cream till very light and fluffy. Sift flour and baking powder together and add alternately with the milk to the first mixture. Fold in the egg whites beaten stiff and the vanilla extract. Bake in three small, or two large, well-greased layer-cake pans for 35-40 minutes. Frost as desired.

DEVIL'S FOOD CAKE

2 eggs, beaten
2 cups brown sugar
1 cup butter
1 cup buttermilk
3 cups cake flour
3 oz chocolate, melted

1 tsp vanilla extract
1 ½ Tbs cinnamon
1 tsp cloves
1 tsp allspice
1 tsp baking soda dissolved in ½ cup of
   boiling water

Preheat oven to 350°F.

Cream butter and sugar and add well-beaten eggs. Add buttermilk, melted choco-late, flour beaten in lightly, vanilla extract, and spices, and, lastly, the boiling water and baking soda. Bake in two greased 9-inch round layer pans at 350°F for 30 minutes, or until toothpick inserted into the center comes out clean. Cool completely. Spread filling between layers (see below) and frost as desired.

FILLING:

2 cups white sugar
1 cup milk
3 oz. chocolate, melted

1 egg yolk
⅓ cup butter
1 tsp vanilla extract

Put all the ingredients except vanilla in a saucepan and place over medium heat. Cook until thick, then beat until creamy, add vanilla extract, and spread on layers.

DUTCH APPLE CAKE

2 eggs
1 ½ cups milk
1 Tbs butter, melted
½ tsp salt
½ cup sugar

2 cups flour
3 tsp baking powder
2 apples, peeled, cored and cut into small
    pieces

Preheat oven to 350°F.

Separate two eggs. Add to the yolks milk, butter, and salt. Sift together flour and baking powder, and add to the wet mixture. Beat quickly, fold in the well-beaten egg whites, and turn into a greased 7 x 11 baking-pan. Cover the top thickly with apple pieces, and dust half a cupful of sugar over the top. Bake for about 45 to 50 minutes, or until the apples are tender. Serve with whipped cream.

Peaches, huckleberries, blackberries, or elderberries may be substituted for the apples.

SPICE CAKE WITH LEMON COCONUT FILLING

4 eggs, beaten
2 cups sugar
1 cup butter
1 cup milk
3 cups cake flour

1 tsp baking powder
½ lb raisins
1 tsp cinnamon
1 tsp cloves
1 tsp allspice

FILLING:

2 cups sugar
2 lemons, juice and grated rind
2 cups grated coconut

1 cup boiling water
1 Tbs cornstarch, dissolved in a little cold
   water

Preheat oven to 350°F.

Cream butter and sugar, and add to well-beaten eggs. Next, add the milk, flour, baking powder, raisins, and spices. Bake in a 9-inch tube pan for one hour, or until the center springs back when touched.

To make the filling, mix sugar, lemons, grated coconut, and water, and bring to boil, then add the cornstarch mixture. Cook until it spins a thread, then beat until creamy and spread between layers.

HOLIDAY SPICED CAKE

⅓ cup butter
1 cup sugar
2 egg yolks
⅔ cup buttermilk
1 ½ tsp cinnamon
¼ tsp ground cloves

¼ tsp mace
1 tsp baking soda
2 cups flour
1 egg white
1 tsp vanilla extract

Preheat oven to 350°F.

Cream the butter, and add the sugar and egg yolks. Mix well. Mix and sift all dry ingredients. Sift and add alternately to butter mixture with buttermilk. Mix in vanilla extract and fold in stiffly beaten egg white. Bake in a greased loaf cake pan, prepared with waxed paper for about 30 to 45 minutes, or until the edges have browned and the center is well-set. Cover with Brown Sugar Icing (see page 179).

Country Kitchen Tip

Never let cake batter sit around before baking. The leavening will begin to escape and your cake may not rise.

LEMON SPONGE CAKE

2 egg yolks
1 cup sugar
1 cup boiling water
1 Tbs lemon juice
1 tsp grated rind lemon

2 egg whites
1 cup flour
1 tsp baking powder
¼ tsp salt

Preheat oven to 350°F.

Beat the yolks until thick, add the sugar gradually, and beat for two minutes. Sift together the flour, baking powder, and salt, and add to the egg and sugar mixture. Add the boiling water, lemon juice, and grated rind. Beat for two minutes. Fold in stiff egg whites. Pour into a greased bundt pan and bake for 30 to 35 minutes.

GINGER CUPCAKES

Yields 12 Cupcakes

1 cup molasses
½ cup boiling water
2 ¼ cup flour
1 tsp baking soda

2 tsp ginger
½ tsp salt
½ cup chopped raisins (optional)
4 Tbs melted butter

Preheat oven to 350°F.

Put the molasses in a bowl and add the boiling water. Sift together the dry ingredients and add to the molasses mixture. Add the melted butter and beat well for two minutes. Add raisins, if desired, and mix. Pour into buttered muffin pans, filling the pans two-thirds full. Bake for about 20 to 25 minutes.

GRAHAM CRACKER CAKE

⅓ cup butter
⅔ cup sugar
2 egg yolks
1 cup milk
2 cups crushed graham crackers

3 tsp baking powder
2 egg whites, beaten
½ tsp ground cinnamon
½ tsp vanilla extract

Preheat oven to 350°F.

Cream the butter, add the sugar, and beat. Add egg yolks and beat another minute or so. In a separate bowl, mix together the dry ingredients. Add to the butter and sugar mixture alternately with the milk. Beat two minutes. Add the vanilla extract. Beat the egg whites until stiff and fold into the batter. Bake in square baking pans for about 25 minutes.

Frost with Confectioner's Sugar Icing (page 180) or simply dust with confectioner's sugar.

CUT-OUT CAKES

½ cup butter
1 cup sugar
8 egg yolks
½ cup milk

1 ¾ cup flour
2 tsp baking powder
2 tsp lemon extract

Preheat oven to 350°F.

Cream together the butter and sugar. Beat the egg yolks until very thick, and add to the first mixture. Sift together the flour and baking powder and add the milk to the butter and sugar mixture alternately with the flour mixture, beating well. After mixing, beat two minutes. Add the lemon extract. Line a jelly roll pan with parchment paper. Pour in the batter until one inch thick. Bake for about 12 minutes. Remove from the oven and, when cool, cut into shapes with cookie cutters. Ice as desired. Leftover bits of cake can be used in a trifle.

LEMON CAKE

1 ⅓ cup sugar   ½ tsp lemon extract
3 eggs   2 cups flour
½ cup water   2 tsp baking powder

Preheat oven to 350°F.

Beat the egg yolks five minutes, add the sugar and beat three minutes. Add the water, lemon extract, flour, and baking powder. Mix thoroughly. Fold in the beaten egg whites very carefully. Bake for about 25 minutes in two greased round layer pans. When cool, spread Lemon Cream Filling between layers (page 164). Frost with Confectioners' Sugar Icing (page 180)

LEMON CREAM FILLING

⅔ cup sugar

⅓ cup flour

½ tsp salt

1 ½ cup milk

1 egg yolk

½ tsp vanilla extract

½ tsp lemon extract

Mix together the sugar, salt, and flour. Gradually add the milk, stirring constantly. Pour into the top of a double boiler, and cook until very thick. Add the egg yolk, vanilla extract, and lemon extract, and cook two minutes. Remove from heat and whisk until creamy and cool.

CHOCOLATE NOUGAT CAKE

4 Tbs butter

⅔ cup sugar

2 squares baking chocolate (16 oz)

2 Tbs sugar

2 Tbs water

1 egg

½ cup milk

1 ⅓ cup flour

2 tsp baking powder

½ tsp baking soda

½ tsp vanilla extract

Preheat oven to 350°F.

In a saucepan, heat the two tablespoons of sugar, water, and chocolate for one minute, stirring constantly. In a mixing bowl, cream together the butter, sugar, egg, and vanilla extract, beating until light and fluffy. Sift together the flour, baking powder, and baking soda, and add alternately to the batter with the milk and chocolate mixture until thoroughly combined. Pour into two well-greased square layer-cake pans. Bake for 20 to 25 minutes, or until toothpick inserted into the center comes out clean. Chocolate cakes burn easily and they should be carefully watched while baking. Ice with White Mountain Cream Icing (page 182).

STRAWBERRY SHORTCAKE

4 cups flour
2 tsp baking powder
2 Tbs butter
1 cup milk

1 Tbs sugar
Strawberries
Whipped cream (for topping)

Preheat oven to 350°F.

Sift flour and baking powder together, then use your fingers to work in the butter until the mixture becomes crumbly. Add the sugar and milk, and mix just until combined. Bake in a greased and floured cake pan for 15 to 20 minutes. Serve hot with sliced strawberries and plenty of whipped cream.

MOCHA ALMOND CAKE

1 ½ cups flour
1 cup sugar
2 eggs
2 cups butter

¾ cup milk
1 ½ tsp baking powder
½ lb shelled almonds

Preheat oven to 350°F.

Brown almonds slightly in oven, grind finely, and mix with a little pulverized sugar. Set aside. Cream together the butter and sugar and add both egg yolks. Sift together the flour and baking powder and add to the butter mixture alternately with the milk. Beat the egg whites until they form stiff peaks and then fold them into the batter. Bake in greased square pans for 10 to 15 minutes. When cool, cut in small squares, butter each piece on all sides, then roll in the mixture of ground almonds and sugar.

SNIPPY DOODLE CAKE

1 cup granulated sugar
1 cup flour
½ cup milk
2 eggs, beaten light

1 Tbs butter
1 Tbs cinnamon
1 ½ tsp baking powder
Extra ¼ cup granulated sugar for dusting

Preheat oven to 350°F.

Cream together the butter and sugar, add the eggs, and beat until light and fluffy. Sift together the flour, baking powder, and cinnamon. Add alternately with the milk to the batter. Mix just until combined. Bake in a greased sheet cake pan for about 15 minutes, then sprinkle granulated sugar on top and return to oven for 10 minutes more.

SUNSHINE CAKE

1 ¼ cups sugar
1 cup flour
7 egg whites
5 egg yolks

1 pinch salt
⅓ tsp cream of tartar
1 Tsp lemon or orange extract

Preheat oven to 350°F.

Sift together the sugarflour, and salt and set aside. Separate the eggs. Beat the yolks until frothy. Beat whites with cream of tartar until stiff peaks form. Add yolks and extract and beat. Fold in the flour. Bake for 40-50 minutes in an ungreased tube or loaf pan.

COFFEE CAKE

1 cup butter

1 cup sugar

1 cup molasses

1 egg

1 cup chopped raisins

1 cup strong brewed coffee

1 tsp baking soda

1 tsp cinnamon

1 tsp vanilla extract

2 ½ cups flour

Preheat oven to 350°F.

Cream together the butter, sugar, egg, and molasses. In a separate bowl, combine the flour, baking soda, and cinnamon. Add to the butter mixture alternately with the coffee, beating after each addition. Add the vanilla extract. Bake in two greased loaf pans for 50 to 60 minutes.

SOUR CREAM NUT LAYER CAKE

2 eggs
1 cup granulated sugar
½ cup sour cream
2 cups flour

½ tsp baking soda
1 tsp baking powder
Pinch of salt

Preheat oven to 350°F.

Beat the eggs until frothy. Add the sugar and sour cream, and continue to beat. Sift together the flour, baking soda, baking powder, and salt, and beat well. Bake in three greased and floured layer cake pans for about 30 minutes, or until a toothpick inserted into the center comes out clean.

FILLING:

1 cup of pecan or walnuts crushed with
    rolling-pin on bread-board
1 egg

¾ cup confectioner's sugar
½ cup sour cream
A few drops of vanilla extract

Beat the egg well, add the sugar and nuts, and, last of all, the sour cream and vanilla extract, stirring just until combined. Once the cake is cool, spread filling between the layers and over the top.

BLUEBERRY CHEESECAKE

PIE SHELL

2 cups graham cracker crumbs   ¼ lb butter, melted
2 Tbs sugar

FILLING

2 Tbs sugar   ¼ cup sour cream
16 oz cream cheese   1 cup blueberry pie filling

Pie shell: Preheat oven to 350°F. Mix ingredients well and line a 9-inch pie pan. Bake for 6 minutes.

Filling: Blend the cream cheese, sour cream, and sugar until smooth. Pour into pie shell. Top with blueberries. Sprinkle sugar on top and bake at 350°F for 5 minutes. Chill and serve.

CIDER CAKE

3 cups flour

2 cups sugar

1 cup butter

3 eggs

½ tsp salt

1 tsp baking soda

1 cup cider

1 tsp cinnamon and allspice, mixed

1 cup raisins or currants, optional

Preheat oven to 350°F.

Cream together the butter and eggs, add the cider, and beat until mixed. In a separate bowl, mix together the flour, sugar, baking soda, salt, and spices. Add to the butter mixture and beat until combined. The dough should be fairly stiff. Add raisins or currants, if desired. Bake in two greased 8-inch round pans for 25 to 30 minutes. Cover with Brown Sugar Icing (page 179).

HONEY CAKES

1 cup sugar
1 ¾ cups honey
1 tsp cloves
½ tsp ginger
1 tsp cinnamon
½ tsp salt

½ tsp nutmeg
¼ tsp pepper
1 tsp anise
1 ½ cups rye flour
1 ½ cups wheat flour

Preheat oven to 350°F.

Sift together flour, spices, and salt. Put honey and sugar in a saucepan and heat until the mixture begins to boil. Pour it on the flour mixture and stir until a thick dough is formed. If necessary, add more honey or flour until the paste is stiff enough to roll. Roll into small balls and place in greased muffin tin. Bake for about 25 minutes, or until toothpick inserted into the center comes out clean. When cool, dip each ball separately in Vanilla Icing (page 179).

SOUR CREAM ICING

¼ cup butter, softened
½ cup sour cream
½ tsp vanilla extract

¼ tsp salt
2 ¾ cup confectioners' sugar

Beat together the butter, sour cream, vanilla extract, and salt. Add the confectioners' sugar gradually, beating after each addition.

MAPLE POURED FONDANT

6 cups confectioner's sugar
½ cup heavy cream

2 tablespoons maple syrup
1 teaspoon maple extract

In a saucepan combine confectioners' sugar, cream, and maple syrup. Stir continuously over medium heat until it reaches 92°F. Remove from heat and add maple extract. Pour over cooled cake.

VANILLA BUTTERCREAM ICING

3 cups confectioners' sugar
1 cup butter

1 teaspoon vanilla extract
1 ½ tablespoons heavy cream

Cream butter and gradually add confectioners' sugar while beating. Add vanilla and cream and continue to beat until smooth. If icing is too thick, add a little more cream.

BROWN SUGAR ICING

1 cup light brown sugar
⅓ cup water
⅛ tsp cream of tartar

1 egg white
½ tsp vanilla extract

Mix the sugar, water, and cream of tartar in a saucepan. Cook until the syrup clicks when a little is dropped in the cold water. Do not stir while cooking. Have the mixture boil evenly but not too fast. Pour gently over the beaten white of the egg. Stir and beat briskly until creamy. Add vanilla extract. Place on the cake. If too hard, add a tablespoon of water.

ORANGE ICING

2 cups confectioners' sugar
1 tsp melted butter

Juice of ½ orange

Beat sugar and butter into the orange juice until stiff enough to hold its shape when spread on the cake.

CONFECTIONER'S SUGAR ICING

2 Tbs heavy cream or milk
½ tsp vanilla extract

1 Tbs simple syrup or maple syrup
1 ½ cup powdered sugar

Mix the heavy cream, vanilla extract, and syrup. Add the sugar until the right consistency to spread. Spread carefully between the layers and on the top. Set aside to cool, and to allow the icing to "set." (More sugar may be needed in making the icing.)

> **Country Kitchen Tip**
> If your icing is too thick to spread, add a splash of milk or water and mix until smooth.

LEMON BETTINA ICING

1 egg white
1 Tbs heavy cream
2 cups powdered sugar

1 tsp vanilla extract
½ tsp lemon extract

Beat the egg white, add part of the sugar. Add the heavy cream, vanilla extract, and lemon extract. Keep beating. Add the rest of the sugar gradually. (A little more sugar may be needed.) Beat the icing till very fluffy and until it will spread without running off the cake.

WHITE MOUNTAIN CREAM ICING

1 cup granulated sugar
⅛ tsp cream of tartar
¼ cup water

1 egg white
½ tsp vanilla extract

In a double boiler, combine the sugar, water, cream of tartar, and egg white together, and beat for about seven minutes, or until stiff peaks form. Remove from heat and add vanilla extract. Beat for another two to three minutes or until frosting can easily be spread.

Index

The Little Book of Country Baking